A Single Lifetime
1936 - 2006

M. R. Howe

Library of Congress Control Number: 2009940477

ISBN: 978-0-940471-83-2

ॐ

Printed and Manufactured in the United States of America
By
California Publishing Company
989 Howard Street
San Francisco, CA 94103

When one knows thee, then alien there is none, then no door is shut. O grant me my prayer that I may never lose the touch of the one in the play of the many.

— Rabindranath Tagore, Gitanjali

A minority of one, a miniscule disturber of the field of first-century Palestine, would alter the course of history.... Cosmos and self, nature and history, belong together.

— David Toolan, At home in the Cosmos

Solitude that is just solitude and nothing else . . . is worthless. True solitude embraces everything, for it is the fullness of love that rejects nothing and no one, that is open to All in All.

— Thomas Merton, April 14, 1966, Easter Thursday

I am only one,

But I am still one.

I cannot do everything,

But still I can do something;

And because I cannot do everything

I will not refuse to do the

something that I can do.

— Edward Everett Hale, for the Lend-a-Hand Society

Table of Contents

Foreword

Birth makes us one, although we are totally dependent. As children, we remain one, even as dependence lessens. We remain one until we surrender at least a part of that oneness to another, or others, as we mature. Over time, oneness may again assume ascendancy.

Oneness has been important in my life. I have found that to be alone is not to be lonely. I have been single throughout my life, but I have seldom, if ever, been lonely. I have seen greater loneliness in people who are with others most of their day and most of their lives. Perhaps we should be less anxious to surrender oneness before we fully appreciate it.

There was a time when, as a single woman, I would have been ignored, even ridiculed. Since there is no longer such a great need to people the world, however, being single might be a more acceptable alternative. If this book shows oneness in a different way, it has achieved its purpose, even though I do not advocate the single lifestyle over any other.

Someone once asked which year of my life I would most like to live over. My response was that I would not have had the strength to live any year over. I have preferred to live each day in the present and continue to hope for the future, which is not to say that I have ignored the past. The past is a great teacher.

In 1936 I was born into two large, extended, close-knit, rural families — my first contact with the world beyond myself. The town was a small coal-mining town, without even a library. Both sides of my immediate family lived in this same town.

One side of the family had an English-Irish, Catholic background. Divisions within that side of the family became deeper when my grandmother died and my grandfather proved incapable of raising their family An unmarried uncle and an unmarried aunt managed to keep the five children together and strengthened the family tie, but not without some disruption and insecurity. At one time I was unaware that I had relatives living just four miles away. The disruption lessened over time, but a sense of security was harder to achieve.

The other side of the family exhibited all of the solidness of Dutch-German, Protestant ancestry, but the Great Depression sharply limited a road construction business and forced the family to turn at least in part to subsistence farming. Not until the coming of the Second World War and the development of strip mining did my mother's family again experience some degree of economic stability beyond subsistence.

Although much of my parents' daily life experience was similar because of the size of the town and the single public school, there was a chasm between the two families that it took years for my parents to bridge, and religion deepened the chasm. My father went off to college; my mother, to business school. It was, again, the Great Depression that increased the difficulty of creating a life away from home. Both returned to the same small town and eventually married.

No one on either side of my immediate family worked in the underground coal mine, on which the local economy was based at the time I was born. Within my lifetime the underground mine closed, leaving only sulphur fumes and slag piles as reminders; now even the fumes are gone. When I was growing up, I knew there were widows whose husbands had died in the mine, and I knew men who took other jobs when the mine finally closed. I never talked with anyone who would have preferred to go back underground, had it even been possible. The risks are still great in underground mines.

Although there was no library in the town, I read anything I could find. By the time I entered the university, where a library was the focal point, it remained somewhat foreign to me. I had so many things I needed to read to catch up that there was little time to read as I had earlier. It is unfortunate that my reading was only loosely guided when I had time to read, and there was not time to focus my reading adequately when it was at last guided. That proved to be both good and bad. I continue to enjoy reading whatever interests me as time permits, but I find it difficult to focus my reading on any one area.

My ignorance of the past was apparent, even at a young age. Perhaps that is why I chose to study history when I entered the university. It seemed to be the only way I could catch up with what was happening in a world of armed conflict, social upheaval, economic imbalance, and technological advance. Such changes have occurred throughout history, and, as in earlier times, lives are changed.

Some years ago, when I was reading Dietrich Bonhoeffer's *Letters and Papers from Prison*, the first sentence struck me and has remained with me. It provides the basic organization for this book: "Ten years is a long time in anyone's life." I never intended to write a book. I just wanted to live the most constructive life I could, one day at a time.

Now I must caution you. As I learned early in my study of history, memory is not always reliable. Perhaps each person who was part of my life remembers their part somewhat differently. This book does set forth what I remember, and perhaps those memories of an earlier time will have some interest for those facing life today.

The First Decade
1936-1946

Memory does not stretch to the earliest years of one's life. I have, upon occasion, wondered if my arrival disturbed the life of my older sister. She had had considerable attention when she was born, for neither side of the family had enjoyed the company of an infant for some time. She was probably too young to realize fully that a second baby would change that, but she might have sensed a difference.

Although I do not remember the day I was born, it was March 15, 1936—the Ides of March—during the St. Patrick's Day flood of that year. At times I was call the "flood" baby since my father said that he came to see me in a canoe. I do not know abut the canoe, but, in looking through Sylvester K. Stevens' *Pennsylvania: Birthplace of a Nation* (New York: Random House, 1964, p. 375), I found March 1936 listed in the "Chronology" as a time of "disastrous flood in Central Pennsylvania." This was not, however, the better-known and more disastrous Johnstown Flood, which killed so many people in 1889. I am not *that* old!

Homes in our small town had few conveniences. We had electricity, but not indoor plumbing. Even the few homes with indoor plumbing had to provide their own water supply. In my home the kitchen was the focus of much of the activity in the house. Water was hauled from a well on the back porch of the house and carried to the kitchen for all purposes: drinking, cooking, washing dishes, washing clothes, bathing, and cleaning.

In the kitchen water was heated and food was cooked on a coal range. We learned very early to avoid the stove for it was always hot. An accident in which a younger sister was burned by boiling water when a pan on the stove overturned drove this lesson home. In summer, when much of the canning and preserving was done, the stove made the kitchen even hotter. In winter, the same stove made the kitchen the most comfortably warm room in the house. And, yes, there was an outhouse where safe drainage was of greater concern than convenience.

Apart from the kitchen, the house had a living room and a dining room at ground level and three bedrooms that accommodated six people on the second level, where a bathroom was added later.

An unfinished attic was used primarily for storage, and, because of extreme temperatures—

cold in winter and hot in summer—there was a basement that remained damp and cool in the hot summer and usually kept the water pipes from freezing in the cold winter. Much of the basement was taken up by the furnace and the coal required to fuel it. When the heating system was changed from coal-fueled hot air heat to coal-fueled hot water heat, the house was more comfortable in winter. Clothes then could be washed in the basement instead of the kitchen. When the weather was bad and washed clothes could not be hung outside to dry, smaller things were dried on a rack in the kitchen, and larger things were dried in the basement, carefully avoiding the dirt, especially from the coal. When oil later replaced coal as fuel, the basement area became cleaner and more useful.

Two years after I was born, I had a younger sister. I cannot provide a clear picture of what her birth meant to anyone else since I was just two years old and, again, memory is vague then. What I do remember is a sense of calamity, sharpened, perhaps, by later accounts of those whose lives were directly affected. The overwhelming sense of calamity remained.

It took some time before a diagnosis of Down's Syndrome had much meaning, but I vaguely remember early efforts to save my younger sister's life. The search for help and advice in such isolated surroundings bordered on catastrophe. Our parents finally located a doctor who diagnosed the more immediate problem: enlarged adenoids were preventing my sister form breathing and eating at the same time—so essential for a baby. The adenoids were removed as soon a possible.

This critical period soon after birth served as a preview of normal childhood illnesses that proved more devastating for my sister as well as other illnesses that were not so normal, such as erysipelas and scarlatina. With the help of concerned family members and doctors, as well as some unorthodox home remedies (cranberry poultices and a cough mixture of kerosene and sugar, among them), my sister survived. Our parents opted always for conventional medical treatment, but, when that failed, they resorted to whatever else presented itself.

This was a time of change for rural medical practice. Doctor's visits to the home became less common and visits to a doctor's office became more common.

Illness represented just one of the difficulties that were to prove constant throughout my sister's life. Our parents came to accept the fact that her development would never be at the normal rate. Their choices at that time were to raise her in the best manner they could or to place her in a state institution far from home in more ways than just distance. They decided to try to provide what they could of a normal home life. Blessed with support from both sides of the family, the long struggle began, and every small step along the way – eating, talking, walking, dressing (tying shoes!) – represented a major achievement. Our father stated the goal as succinctly as I have ever heard it: The family could not conform to her; she had to conform to the family. And, in spite of sometimes severe difficulties for both her and the family and somewhat less than total success, the goal remained.

None of these experiences seemed as critical at the time as the Second World War. It overshadowed everything. Four uncles and one aunt served in the military, and war news and activity intruded on life at home and at school. Relatives appeared in uniform and then left those at home to worry about them. There were unusual and, at that time, lengthy trips to a distant train station in Altoona; groceries and gasoline were rationed; newspaper accounts and radio news broadcasts assumed importance; and there were bond drives. In what must have been an effort to get rural children involved, we were asked to collect milkweed pods. I am still not sure why, but I hope they helped.

In our remote rural area, the rationing of groceries and gasoline seemed to create the most inconvenience. Mother's parents observed their Golden Wedding Anniversary during the war years. Any celebration was in doubt because of the shortages and rationing, but, being a small town, people gathered together enough ration books to get the supplies needed, and it seemed that the whole town participated.

Also, the last of my sisters was born during the war. She was very welcome, to me, because she represented one more ration book, especially the extra sugar coupons. Television had not yet appeared to educate us about the miracle of birth or to show us the horror of war. The radio and movies did, however, increase awareness.

Finally, the war ended. Travel became easier, water was piped into our homes to allow for indoor plumbing, and war shortages eased. Attention turned to peacetime concerns.

My older sister and I had begun school during the war. A single building contained the public school through the twelfth grade. The only other building even remotely connected to the school was the gymnasium, which was just across the road. Students from smaller elementary schools in smaller towns entered the system at the upper grade levels. Teachers through the lower grades were primarily women who had completed at least two years of education beyond high school. Many were unmarried.

My older sister and I were separated in age by just eleven months. We were not twins, but we were considered to be the same age. This may have held back my sister. It frequently left me running to catch up. We did most things together since few children lived close to our home and a number of the children who went to school with us depended on a school bus for transportation. They ate lunch at school, but we went home for lunch.

Mother always said I was a quiet child, and my early years reflected that. One significant moment in my life was the day I learned to read. From that day on, reading was a great pleasure for me. As I mentioned before, there was no library in our town. The county library provided a bookmobile that served the school. It also came in the summer, and I was only limited by the number of books I could carry. I was never able to carry enough to last until the bookmobile returned, and I appreciated books people gave me from their attics or as gifts.

In class I usually chose to sit in the front of the room, and, when our father pointed out birds in the sky, passing airplanes, or the ball at ballgames, I soon learned that I was supposed to see them, and so I did – sort of. I was not much interested in sports since it is hard to keep one's eye on a ball one could not really see. The summer before I entered second grade, I fell so often that my knees did not heal until Mother poured peroxide on them regularly to speed the healing. When I entered third grade, school subjects became more difficult, and one day, because the teacher was unable to get multiple copies of a test, she wrote the questions on the blackboard. I answered every question – wrong. Since this was the first test I had ever failed, I was upset. At lunch I told my parents that I did not see the questions right. Because this had not happened before, they felt something was different. They asked my older sister to explain this to my tough and skeptical teacher.

As a result, I soon went for an eye examination, and I received my first pair of glasses. Mother was with me in the doctor's office, and, for the first time that I was aware of, I really saw her face. Upon leaving the doctor's office, I found out that it was possible to see the separate leaves on trees from a distance. It was a whole new world!

A couple of years later the doctor giving physical examinations to my class in school took Mother aside and told her that my eyes needed more attention. This was an increased burden for our parents. The closest specialist was located in the college town twenty-seven miles away. This does not seem far today, but then it meant travel through the mountains in an older automobile that only my father could drive. It proved an even greater financial burden, for everyone in the family except our father needed glasses. The doctor would not even give me glasses before he took me, accompanied by my father, to Philadelphia to be sure something more serious was not affecting my vision. Fortunately the problems could be corrected by normal methods.

I have never minded wearing glasses – perhaps because I needed them so badly. The few days I did not have them, when the lenses needed to be repaired or replaced, made me much more unhappy. Once, when both my older sister and I were waiting for new glasses to arrive, we were very disagreeable. When the glasses finally arrived at the doctor's office, both pairs were broken. Perhaps we deserved the longer wait!

The doctor even examined the eyes of our handicapped sister and determined that she also needed glasses. When she was confronted by a full-sized eye chart, and the doctor tried to find the right lens by the somewhat tedious trial-and-error method, he became concerned about the results he was getting. He then inserted a black lens, and, in spite of the fact that she could not see it, she read the line perfectly – from memory. He was not the only doctor whose patience she was to try, but she must have realized that she was able to see better with glasses. Wearing them was not a problem for her, either.

Another memory from my younger years was of my older sister's and my long hair. My sister had long braids, and I had long curls. Our hair had not been cut since we were born since our father preferred that it be long. I am not sure what Mother thought, but I am sure that she had neither the time nor the energy to take care of my hair, especially after our youngest sister was born.

One day Mother, who did not drive, and an aunt (my father's sister), who did drive, took me to get my hair cut. I do not think they told my father. They did ask me if it was all right to have it cut, but I am afraid I did not know much about it beyond the arrangement I had with Mother when she was combing it: I would hold it near my head while she pulled the comb through to the bottom; it hurt less that way.

After my hair was cut, I could take care of it myself. But how it was cut affected how easy it was to manage. My first haircut did not make the task of managing it particularly easy; nor have succeeding ones. Much later in my life I resorted to cutting it myself. I do not like it too long *or* too short.

During this same decade I learned another of life's lessons. One of our aunts arranged to take my older sister and me to the neighboring town, and this was something we looked forward to. On the way I learned how quickly plans can change. The car swerved off the road into a swamp. I have no memory of what caused the car to swerve or of how we got from the swamp to the hospital. My first memory was of being carried from a car to my bedroom by Papa (what he preferred to be called), and I remember, more specifically, that the bandage around my head unwound and troubled me in the middle of the night. Details had to be filled in the next day.

I was a healthy child. When my older sister's tonsils were removed, Mother asked the doctor to remove mine as well. The doctor did not want to do this because I had not had any problem. The next year I missed about thirty days of school with a sore throat. There was no further argument. Since I had been around when my sister's tonsils were removed, I proved a fast learner. I recovered quickly enough to leave the hospital the same day as the operation, which was not so common then. I do not think I missed a full day of school for health reasons throughout my remaining school years except for the multiple times I had measles.

I would like you to leave this period of my life knowing that there were some really special moments in each of the years. First, there were annual carnivals in the neighboring town, and I loved Ferris wheels, merry-go-rounds, and other rides that were not as terrifying as rides have become. Then, in a similar vein, there was the county fair, also an annual event in which there were carnival rides, exhibits, prize animals, horse races, and food booths. Occasionally we would stay for the evening shows. The thirteen-mile trip to the county seat was not as easy then, especially in a one-seat Ford, but the trip and the fair were exciting.

Perhaps more than any other annual event, however, the holidays were important. Except for one year, we were at our grandparents for Thanksgiving dinner. And then there was Christmas.

Since we did not eat Christmas dinner at our own home, our dining room table was the site of our Christmas presents. Each of my sisters and I had a corner of the table, and we had a pile of gifts to open by the big day. Our handicapped sister had only one major wish: that her pile of gifts be the tallest. The gifts did not have to be expensive, and the war influenced what could be obtained in the earlier years. But opening gifts was always exciting.

My older sister and I were the first to be disabused about Santa (which I later preferred to think about as the Santa in you and me, from a poem titled "Santa Claus," by Leigh Hanes). We could then go to Midnight Mass and help decorate the tree after our younger sisters were asleep.

One thing bothered me toward the end of the preparations. We had a cardboard crèche that had to be reassembled each year, and it sort of wore on my father's nerves since he was tired by then. I asked if we could get a crib with free-standing figures, but our parents said that we could not afford that. I then asked if it would be possible to have a set of Lincoln logs. That was possible, and so I constructed a building from them. Then, each of the times I went to the 5 & 10 cent store I bought some really inexpensive figures until I finally had a crèche that our parents kept and I still have. It made Christmas both easier and more meaningful.

The Second Decade
1946-1956

Much of my life early in this decade was spent at school. The school day began at 9:00 a.m. and lasted until 4:00 p.m., with an hour in the middle of the day for lunch. As I moved through the higher grades into high school, more of my teachers were either men or women, married with families. One had served in the navy during the war, and he advanced through several grades as a teacher at the same time I did as a student. This meant he was my only teacher through three of my first eight years. I respected all of my teachers, but he holds a special place in my memories. When I reached high school in the ninth grade, I learned what it was to move from one classroom to another and to have more than one teacher each day.

In high school the curriculum was divided to accommodate students preparing for college and students entering the workforce from high school. My choice of curriculum was not difficult. My parents had stressed the benefits of higher education since I had been born. There was some opportunity to interchange courses, but this was restricted by the availability of teachers and class size. When I wanted to learn to type, for example, there was some difficulty obtaining permission because the typing class was full. This was finally resolved by the hiring of a second teacher for business-related subjects.

Our parents accepted the fact that their handicapped daughter would not be able to enter school at the normal age, for there was no special education at that time. Over time, however, she learned to talk, walk, and dress herself. When she was eight years old, our parents asked that she be admitted to school. They were told that the teachers would have to agree to accept her as a pupil. The remote, rural nature of the school was its own blessing, and the teachers, most of whom knew our parents, agreed to accept her. The teachers, most of whom I had had earlier, were experienced and extraordinarily skilled in presenting basic education to children with few learning advantages. Our sister was held over almost every year she attended school. This helped her learn how to read, write, and spell at her own pace, and she learned how to do all three things well, but arithmetic remained a mystery.

It might seem surprising, but she made good friends along the way. It was our youngest sister, however, who was the greatest aid, for they grew up together. The older learned from the younger until, over time, the younger progressed past the older, with the older leaving school after the seventh grade.

What our parents gained for our handicapped sister through the school, they lost through the Church. Our pastor refused her communion, and so, for a time, we climbed over her each week as we went for communion – leaving her alone in the pew.

We were far from the center of the diocese, and it did not occur to our parents to go beyond the pastor with their request. Mother did, however, read in the Catholic paper about other children with problems who did receive communion. When relatives from Mother's family, who were also Catholic and lived nearer the center of the diocese, were visiting, Mother mentioned that she did not understand why my sister could not also receive communion. They suggested that our parents visit the newer and younger assistant bishop, who had helped their son by suggesting that he leave the Catholic school and attend the public school where more of the classes might interest him. Our family went on what was then a long trip to meet with the assistant bishop. Soon after we returned, our pastor was transferred. Not only did our sister join us for communion, but she was soon confirmed.

Speaking of confirmation, I now go back to a somewhat earlier time when my older sister and I were attending classes in preparation for confirmation. Our father went to the priest to ask that we be confirmed together since confirmation was only held every three years. In Papa's mind, the priest agreed – until just before confirmation day. He then said that he did not feel that I was mature enough to be confirmed. For my father, this was a violation of trust. He insisted that my older sister be held over as well, and at the same time he resigned as an usher at the church. Three years later we were both confirmed, but Papa did not resume his duties as usher.

There was one other important aspect of my confirmation. An aunt, who had recently married into our family and had a young baby, agreed to make my dress while I watched her infant. When I look at pictures from that day, the dress is special, and it has become more so since my aunt sadly died of early-onset Alzheimer's disease when she was rather young.

Struggles like these make me aware of how difficult it is to be a parent. My early childhood was filled with the tensions and frustrations of our sister's difficulties, but these and other problems were eased by caring parents.

I recall that my early years were particularly hard for our mother. Today I am even more aware of the difficulties she faced while raising a family where there were so few conveniences. She was an older parent who had three children in four years, one of them handicapped.

Our father was the postmaster in our small town. He worked long hours, six days a week during the earlier years, and was home for three meals each day, as we were. He also shared with his sisters some of the concerns for their older brother and the aging uncle who had assumed responsibility for their family, as well as the presence in the small town of an aging father who had not assumed that responsibility.

Mother was equally loyal to her family. It is not always easy to have so many relatives in one small town. It seemed that someone always needed care and that someone's feelings were always being hurt because there were so many opinions about everything.

Within any town, faith in its broadest (and narrowest) sense is important. The most concrete manifestation of faith is most often found in houses of worship, whether the town be large or small. Perhaps churches assume greater importance in small towns because there are fewer activities and fewer distractions.

Where I grew up, there were two major established churches: Methodist and Roman Catholic. Eastern European people who moved to the town because of the mine were incorporated into the Catholic Church, which also served Irish and Italian immigrants. There was a social as well as a theological divide between the two churches. The Methodist church served the better-established citizens. Apart from regular services, the Methodists held some revival meetings, and the Catholics held some missions. The few places the two groups had even passing acquaintance, apart from school and everyday life, were church dinners and picnics. Religious division was even evident in the school: which Bible to use, the ending of the Our Father, choice of commencement speaker. The ecumenical spirit was weak in my youth.

Mother had been a devout Methodist. She converted to Catholicism after she and my father married because she did not want her children to feel divided in what she considered the most important part of one's life – one's faith. As a child I felt that faith involved much drudgery. I was not yet mature enough to separate the letter of church law from its spirit. I was fortunate, for my parents were of great help distinguishing letter from spirit.

In one instance, I was attending a mission at our church when a missionary stated that one could only go to heaven if one was a member of our faith. I was so upset that I told my father I was not going back for the rest of the mission week. He asked why I was so upset, and I told him that the priest had indicated that half of my family was going to hell. My father simply asked if I believed that, and I emphatically said "no." If that was the case, my father asked what difference it made. I reluctantly finished the mission week, but, what was more important, I had learned to respect my own conscience.

I remember another time, in this instance related to school, when one of the boys spit on me. I still do rot know why, but the teacher was upset and maintained that it was only fair that I do the same to the boy, and she gave me little choice. I was fortunate that I did not know how to spit very well. When I told my father about this, he asked me if two wrongs made a right. The fact that this was a question and not a statement preserved the authority of the teacher, but caused me to evaluate the situation for myself. I think my father's mind and mine were closely attuned, and this question has remained with me even when the conclusion is less obvious.

At the beginning of my teenage years, my life changed. I was asked if I wanted to help Mother's sister, who was badly crippled with arthritis. She was maintaining their family home, just down the street from our family home, for her father and several brothers. The woman who helped through the day was not able to stay through the dinner hour because she had a son who needed her. An older woman who had been coming and staying through the dinner hour was becoming less able to deal with the irregular hours of my uncles' work and home life. I agreed to do this, and my life changed greatly.

Instead of coming home from school in the late afternoon, I stopped to help my aunt get the evening meal. It was about 7:00 p.m. before we had eaten and everything was cleared away. I realized that I needed to get my homework done, and the time after 7:00 p.m. seemed best for accomplishing this since I was expected back at my aunt's in about an hour to stay with my grandfather while my aunt was out. What I had not realized was that my father would expect me to come home during that hour. He was not pleased that I was away from home so much, and so I lost the earlier time to do my homework.

When I returned to my aunt's home at about 8:00 p.m., the television was on for my grandfather, a neighbor, and my handicapped sister to watch. Television sets were not as common at that time. Perhaps I should have resisted watching and gone to the kitchen to finish my homework, but I could not always resist the temptation. Homework delayed or postponed often had to be finished when I reached home later in the evening. It was never neglected or ignored, but the late hour when it was completed made early morning rising even more difficult than it often is in the teen years.

This pattern became so set that I did not realize how difficult my divided life had become. I continued to read as much as I could, and I was never without a book to read during my spare moments, even though, by the time I reached high school, subjects became more complicated; assignments, more demanding; and time, more pressing.

There were changes at home as well. My older sister and I no longer shared a bedroom with our younger sisters. Instead, the two of us shared a separate room. Perhaps because I was home so little or perhaps because we had different life experiences, we were developing distinctively different personalities.

My memory of my first year in high school is vague. It was somewhat of an adjustment, but life did not change very much. By the second year, things did change. In the first year my quiet and non-revolutionary class had chosen a president that they were unhappy with by the second year.

Earlier class presidents had exhibited stronger, more diverse personalities, and my class decided it needed a different class president. I was surprised to find myself the new class president, which I saw as being more unsettling than empowering.

I was not a dominant or popular figure. I would characterize myself as more of a "loner." And, however I characterized myself, I was alone much of the time in relation to school activities. I did try to see that the class was treated fairly and in the manner that other classes had been treated. This was not always easy. As president, I was expected to attend certain functions of upper classes so that I would know what should be done as our class moved along. As a sophomore I attended the prom – alone.

In my junior year the principal decided that no class time should be devoted to decorating the gymnasium for the prom. As the class rep-resentative, I had to go to his office and explain that, since so many of our students came to school by bus and they could not stay after school to decorate, there was no way to trim the gymnasium and make it suitable for a dance unless the class could work on it during school hours. I was not able to secure release from classes, but I was at least able to get class members released from their study periods. That was my major contribution to the success of the prom since I had almost no free study periods. I did not see the results until the night of the prom, at which I attended the dinner and welcomed the senior class. The gymnasium was appropriately transformed by the more creative members of the class, and I attended the dance briefly. By my senior year, the decorations were the responsibility of the lower class, and I simply had to acknowledge their efforts and thank them.

In my junior year the economic difficulties that permeated the area entered the school arena. Every other year the school arranged a trip to Washington, D.C., for juniors and seniors in high school. Since many students had not had much opportunity to travel, this was a long-anticipated event. Early in the planning stage, one student made clear that he could not go. The class worked diligently and successfully to raise the money that would allow him to make the trip. Then, almost on the day we were to leave, some of my classmates told me that one of the girls in the class had been given a choice as to whether she got a dress for the prom or went on the trip. She decided that the dress was more important. Some in the class felt that, since we had raised funds for one person, it was not fair to have him go and not her. If we had had more time, perhaps a different way could have been found, but, based on the situation, the lack of time, and the young woman's choice, it was decided that things should remain as they originally had been planned. She was unable to go. At one point in my life I said I wanted to be the first woman president. At this point in my life, I changed my mind.

When one is with peers, the appropriateness of clothes assumes greater importance. It was something that I could relate to because, when I attended the prom as a guest in my sophomore year, I wore my best dress, not a gown. When I attended the prom in my junior year, I again decided to wear a street-length dress that I would be able to wear more than one time. I ordered my dress from a catalogue, and it was dressier than usual. By the time I was a senior, my sister was in college. Money was not available for a new dress for the prom, and Mother asked if I could wear the dress I had worn the year before. She said she would try to see that I got a new dress for graduation. I agreed that a dress I could only wear once was impractical, and the dress I had would be all right, for I was again going alone.

I wish the story of the graduation dress had ended there, but it did not. When I began to look for a dress, I was not able to find one that fit or that I liked. Mother knew that the aunt that I had been helping over the years and another of her sisters were to attend a meeting in a nearby city. Mother suggested that I ask them if they would have time to look for a dress there. They explained to me that there would not be enough time to do this. When I told my quiet mother that, she left our house to talk with them. When they returned from the meeting, my aunts had found me a dress unlike any I had ever seen or could have found near home. What was more surprising was that it fit perfectly. I have no idea what changed their minds, but I gained a keen appreciation of Mother's quiet strength.

I am moving through my high school years rather quickly. This does not mean they were easy years. They were as difficult and complicated as the growing-up years are for most young people. Mine were marked by my family responsibilities, my position as class president, my standing in the class, and my parents' expectation that I would go on to college. Papa was a college graduate, and Mother had been educated beyond high school. Neither saw much opportunity where we lived, especially for women.

The fact that my sister had entered a university in a nearby city perhaps provided a preview of what I faced. Her first year was difficult, and she suggested that I attend the same school she was attending. When she sought scholarship aid that might have made this possible, however, the scholarship office at her school maintained that, if our parents could even envision having two students enrolled at the same time, we did not need scholarship aid. Little did they know (or care) how great the sacrifice was!

Our parents bought little for themselves. One morning when I came downstairs, I saw Papa putting ink on his dark blue overcoat to cover the worn area. This is burned in my memory, along with the time, somewhat later, when Mother's camel-colored coat showed wear. We bought some camel-colored material, and I separated the threads so that I could darn the worn spot. Try as I might, the repair was not good. I had never seen our parents in any other dress coats, even though we lived in a climate where warm clothing was needed during harsh winters. When one of our aunts entered the service during the Second World War, she did not wear the shoes that the army provided. She sent them home, and Mother wore them.

While our grandfather was still living, he would get overripe fruit from the grocery store, and his family preserved it for the long winter when fresh fruits and vegetables were difficult to obtain. One benefit of the victory garden that Papa grew during and after the war was that vegetables could be grown and preserved. This became easier with the advent of the freezer. What my father planted, Mother, my sisters, and I picked. The quality was outstanding, but it destroyed any joy I might ever feel about growing things. I do, however, still look for fresh produce when I can find it.

In time hot lunches became available at school for minimal cost, but we still did not eat there. Since we could walk to school, it was money we did not need to spend.

In turn, I worked hard to maintain my grades. It was clear that going to a school of any size would not be easy with my small-school, small-town background. What was taught was taught well, and I am grateful. But the wider world was still pretty much of a mystery to me. This hit me with great suddenness as I faced the end of my high school years. After my sister's efforts to obtain scholarship aid failed, the best path that seemed open to me was to attend a large state university not too far from home. Tuition was much less, but even that would not be easy financially.

When I graduated from high school, there were forty-two in my class: fifteen young men and twenty-seven young women. Small as it was, it was considerably larger than the class that had graduated with my parents, largely because of consolidation with neighboring smaller schools.

For the first time in my life I was facing great change, and this became ever more apparent.

My last year in high school was different. That difference seemed to color things that occurred throughout the year.

My older sister and I had attended classical music concerts in a neighboring town. When she left for school, my parents decided that I should still go to the concerts, even though I was no longer taking piano lessons (which even my piano teacher had said was a waste of money). My youngest sister, an aunt, and a friend of my aunt's went to the concert, and my aunt's friend drove. Afterward she asked if she could drop my sister and me at the main road since there were no lights on our street and she, being older, was reluctant to turn her car around where it was dark and unfamiliar. I had walked the short distance to our house many times, and this was no problem. She left us at the corner and drove on.

As we started up the road toward home, we passed the "beer garden" on the corner just as a man emerged from the side entrance. Something inside me urged caution. The only thing I could think to do was to enter the driveway across the street, where the aunt that I helped each day lived. I hoped the man would get in his truck and drive off if we were out of sight. When we walked back to the street after a brief time, he was still there. I knew my aunt's home was never locked, but no one was awake. I went in and called home. Papa had also been asleep, and he was not anxious to come out to meet us, but he said he would come. My next worry was to allow him enough time to start down the road but not to get to where the truck was parked. Even though I knew no one would believe me if the person had already driven away, I also realized the possible danger if my father confronted the person. My sister and I waited a few minutes and then started out the driveway again. The truck was still there, but I could see Papa approaching. We started toward him. When the man in the truck saw him, he finally drove off. Although people believe living in a rural area is safer than living in an urban area, I had learned that no place is truly "safe."

As my last year of high school was drawing to a close, our parents' financial struggle was weighing on me, along with the problems my older sister was having in adjusting to university life. The only worlds I had much acquaintance with were home, school, and church. As minds sometimes do when life changes, my mind traveled back to a day when two nuns visited our town, with one specifically pointing me out as a likely candidate for the convent. I became concerned that, if I should go on to college and decide that I had a religious vocation, my parents would have spent money they could ill afford. I felt that I had to decide this before I could enroll in college. Entering the religious life was not something I wanted to do, but life had offered me little to counterbalance religious experience. As the year progressed, the strain of deciding what to do next increased, and I did not feel comfortable sharing this worry with anyone else.

My faith ultimately helped me make the decision. There was a very special day when my life suddenly seemed to open before me, and what I realized was that I would have other responsibilities over time, and what would be needed to assume those responsibilities was to proceed each day to gain the knowledge and the strength that would be required for them. From that time onward, I was able to devote all of my efforts toward going on to school. Confidence in the wisdom of this decision grew over time, along with the uncertainty about what I would be doing with my life.

For our graduation ceremony, we were responsible for making the auditorium look more inviting. The class met early in the day for practice, and the advisor sent some students out to look for flowers that people might be willing to donate. He warned them that they had to return by 2:30 p.m., for he had an appointment that he could not break.

Where we lived in the mountains, flowers were not easy to find in late spring. The students who went looking for flowers were not back by exactly

2:30, and the teacher locked the auditorium door and left. I did not leave because I knew that, if the students found many flowers, it was because the donors were generous in allowing them to take so many of the few then in bloom. It seemed wrong not to use the flowers, but there seemed no way to get them into the auditorium since the door was locked.

I had no idea what to do, but the students did soon return with lovely flowers. It occurred to me that, when we were in the lower grades, the windows of those rooms were not locked. If one student stood on another student's shoulders, he might be able to raise the window and enter the first-grade room. It would then be simple to cross the hall to the auditorium and open the door from the inside. In those days there was no alarm, and there is still no local police force. The problem was whether I should ask two boys to do this and rely on them to crawl through the window, walk through the first-grade room touching nothing, and open the auditorium door. If they could do this, we could place the flowers where they were to go and clean up.

Then we could close the door, which would lock automatically, and we could all leave. Two boys said they thought they could get in the window, and they agreed to touch nothing before opening the auditorium door. We finished decorating and left, closing the door behind us.

The auditorium looked lovely for graduation. The advisor asked how we had done it, but I told him that he did not want to know. As for me, I regretted that a day that should have been rewarding had to be accompanied by a small sense of guilt. But there were no regrets.

This was not the only disconcerting aspect of my graduation, and, because it is such an important milestone, these memories last a long time. Through school I had not encountered overt prejudice against women. I had been chosen class president, and I had earned my place as valedictorian of the class. Neither side of the family harbored such a prejudice, and both sides of the family did as much as they could to educate their children, boys or girls.

Just before graduation my parents asked our parish priest to join our family for dinner. He knew that my older sister was at a university and that I hoped to attend one as well. As we concluded the meal, I was shocked to hear him say that he considered it a waste of money to educate a girl. He was a good priest, and my parents respected him. I am just glad they were not influenced by an opinion they did not share.

There is a certain element of competition in high school because grades earned determined class ranking. In our small town graduation was perhaps the only time one was rewarded for one's standing. The valedictorian and the salutatorian were the two people with the highest grades, and they addressed the audience assembled for the ceremony. I was to deliver the valedictory address.

We had sent away for sample speeches, and I chose one based on Robert Frost's "Mending Wall" that was concerned with neighbors and fences. I think it was more mine than the sample speech by the time I finished rewriting it. It focused more on a song from *South Pacific*: "You've Got to Be Taught to Hate and Fear." I was glad that I was able to convince our advisor that I needed the speech in front of me since my ability to memorize was poor for reasons that continue to elude me.

After graduation the next hurdle was college. Preparation for college was simpler than it is today. Since I was going to the state university, I did not have to take examinations to enter, and I chose to enter the School of Liberal Arts. Then, on a postcard containing perhaps six choices, they asked me to choose a major field for study. The only two areas that I felt qualified to consider were literature and history. In spite of my love of reading, most of it would not have been considered serious literature.

Realizing that I wanted to know more about the past as a basis for all else, the choice was easier: history.

A lingering cold made my first days at the university more difficult, but the university provided a release as well as a challenge. When I entered, there was a brief period of orientation that was helpful for me since I came from such a small, rural school, but my real orientation lasted through my first two years. For the first time in my life I was free to think about my own needs. It took some time for me to make that adjustment. This did not mean that I forgot about home. I was still too close geographically and emotionally to be completely separate. I was expected, however, to schedule my own life, and I stumbled through the first two years, just happy to have survived. My history courses – ancient (first semester), medieval (second semester), early European and early United States (third semester), and modern European and modern United States (fourth semester) – completed the required survey courses for my major area of study. By the time I entered my third year, I had gained the confidence to express myself when it was necessary and could choose among upper-level courses that were both more absorbing and more demanding.

One of the familiar things I brought from home was my faith. I was not at school very long before I realized how important it was to continue to learn more about it as a counterbalance to the tremendous amount I was learning about everything else. Since the university was large but located in a very small town, there were several thousand Catholic students and a church that held about two hundred people. The pastor was terminally ill, and he had one assistant – a young priest just out of the seminary. The church could not accommodate the student body, and some students used this as an excuse to avoid church services. If (as I was given to understand) the bishop was not concerned because he felt that we should not be at a state university, I am grateful that the university was concerned and allowed Sunday mass to be celebrated in the school auditorium. There was a Newman Club, and the university was building a small interfaith chapel on campus – the gift of a former president honoring his wife who died while he was serving as president. I can say with some authority that the situation improved while I was in school there and has improved greatly since then.

A professor of art, who was also a convert to Catholicism, was generous enough to conduct weekly discussions for Catholic students on campus. He nurtured an appreciation of my faith that has remained throughout my life. For some years after I left the university and until his death, we exchanged greetings at Christmas. His cards were works of art that I still treasure.

Over these years, Thanksgiving and Christmas changed even more for me. Since I helped my aunt after school and on vacations, I knew where things were in her kitchen. This meant that I was helpful when preparing holiday meals.

My aunt loved Christmas, and she once said she wished every day was Christmas. Because it was difficult for her to move around, she shopped as opportunities presented themselves, often at home and throughout the year. Everything she bought was placed in a small room next to her bedroom. Different members of the family helped her sort things out according to what they felt was wanted, needed, or could be used. The gifts were not wrapped, but put in decorated bags with names on them. After Christmas we were allowed to choose from the things that were left in the room, and I still have some of my "after Christmas" gifts.

When I was at the university, there was a particularly nice gift shop downtown. One day I found a Hummel grouping of the Christmas scene (Mary, Joseph, and baby). I bought it as a Christmas gift for my aunt, and I told her she could now enjoy Christmas every day. When my aunt died, my mother returned it to me. I hope my aunt knows that I am still enjoying Christmas every day.

The Third Decade
1956-1966

When I entered my third year at the university, I discovered the wonderful world of elective courses. Because I was a history major, I had joined the History Round Table earlier. Through this group I became acqainted with most of the undergraduate and graduate students majoring in history, as well as most of the faculty members in the history department. I also held various offices and helped arrange regular meetings. I welcomed the increased responsibility and social contacts beyond the classroom, which was helpful when considering which courses and which professors to choose.

One concern remained throughout my college years, however. I knew that I had to be prepared to earn a living when I graduated. By the time I entered my junior year, I had thought through what I needed to do to be able to teach. I wanted to continue my major in history, and I could not do that in the education department, which considered history to be part of the broader area of social studies. I carefully planned my schedule to include all of the prerequisites for teaching, much to my advisor's dismay. When I registered for my senior year, the people conducting registration questioned my request to go student teaching over eight weeks, claiming that I did not have the required courses. I insisted that they check the catalogue and established that I did have those courses.

I had already asked the professor who was conducting the undergraduate history seminar, which required that history majors write a senior paper, about this. He felt that, if I could produce an acceptable paper in the eight weeks following student teaching, I would receive course credit. The eight weeks of student teaching was rewarding for many reasons: practical experience, independent living away from home and campus, work with a campus coordinator and a master teacher, a first contact with urban living and the encounter with students of varying abilities at the eighth-grade level in a suburban community. I did well grade-wise, and I was able to assess the experience realistically.

I was told that the School of Education at the university made it impossible for anyone else to qualify for student teaching as I had, but I do not know that this was true then or would still be true today. When I returned to campus, I worked on my senior paper, which was a study of why Theodore Roosevelt appears on the Mount Rushmore monument ("Two Men and a Mountain"). This question arose after an earlier trip to the Black Hills with an uncle and two cousins.

I was still uncertain what I would do after graduation, but I did know that I could be certified to teach in the public school. I was told that I would probably not be able to teach history there because, at that time, most of the teachers assigned to teach history were athletic coaches accredited in the more general area of social studies. This had been true in my high school. I liked teaching, but I also realized that I had little in common with younger people and that I was no disciplinarian.

As graduation neared, I was walking down the mall one day when one of my professors met me. He asked what I planned to do after graduation. I explained that I was not yet sure, and he asked if I had thought of going to graduate school. I explained that this was out of the question since I could not ask my parents to contribute further to my education. He then introduced the possibility of obtaining a graduate assistantship if I were willing to work part-time and, therefore, take two years to complete the work for a master's degree. The opportunity to return to the university for graduate work satisfied my desire for continued learning from people whose company I respected and enjoyed.

Graduate school opened another facet of learning for me: seminars. I enjoyed the smaller classes and the different way they were conducted. More papers had to be written, and there were the ultimate efforts: a master's thesis and comprehensive examinations. My major areas of study were United States history from 1789 to 1860 and European history from 1400 to 1815. My minor was in early American literature.

As I worked my way through the two-year period, I learned more about history in the two areas of specialization, and I understood why my choice of history as my major rather than literature was a wise one. As I moved through the years as a graduate student, I also learned more about myself. The first year I stayed in a room off campus, and the second year I shared an apartment with another graduate student in history. Between the two school years, I joined my older sister in Washington, D.C., which was my first real exposure to life in a large city.

I had written a letter requesting a summer job at a nonprofit professional association focused on history. My letter was misfiled and not answered, but I visited the office to inquire about the letter. By chance, there was an opening in one of the offices for a secretary, and I was hired for the summer.

This was the first time I had been gainfully employed, and I enjoyed my work at the association for so many reasons. A whole new world opened up, but I still planned to return to the university to finish the final year of my master's program. The executive secretary of the association made it possible for me to do some research on my master's thesis ("John Quincy Adams and the Georgia Indian Problem") at the National Archives. I was curious because Adams seemed to be the only president who expressed concern about the way the Indians were being treated.

When I left the association that summer, I had begun to realize that I would be ready to leave graduate school when I received my master's degree. I felt that to specialize further in history was, for me, to learn more about less. I needed to move beyond school – but not before obtaining my degree.

The man that I had worked for at the association asked me if I would like to attend an annual meeting that was to be held in Chicago that year, just after Christmas. I returned to the university that fall, and, just after Christmas with my family, I left on the train for Chicago, where I was met by friends I had made earlier at the association. Over the course of the meeting, where I was with and occasionally met professional historians whose works I had only read or used previously, a pattern was established that was to carry over the next decade of my life. For, it was at this meeting that I was asked if I wanted to work at the association when I completed work for my degree. This was a great incentive to complete my graduate work when I returned to the university. I had to finish my thesis and take comprehensive examinations.

I had been working on my thesis, and I had taken some of the courses needed to prepare for the examinations. The second year of graduate school presented me with some hard choices, however, and I did not, perhaps, make the wisest ones on the path I had set for myself. In one case, I had to choose between a course in European history taught by a professor I liked and a course in American history taught by the professor who had been my ideal as a teacher and who had inspired me both as an undergraduate and a graduate student. My background in European history was weaker, making the choice even more difficult. I opted for the course in American history. Perhaps that is one reason why I failed the comprehensive examination in European history and had to retake it before I could graduate.

Also, I had completed the research for my thesis, and I felt that I could write it after the spring break. When I handed it to my advisor, he felt it was too short, and he felt there would be some objection to thanking a friend from the association who had looked it over when she visited me at the university. I felt that I had said what I wanted to say, and I objected to lengthening it just for the sake of lengthening it. And, if there was any objection to my friend's having looked at it and having made some minor suggestions, I was prepared to submit the earlier version. I departed for the graduate school office to work out these matters, and I was fortunate that these concerns were not shared there. They approved the thesis, and, after I finally passed the European part of the comprehensive examination, I was awarded my degree at the summer graduation. I did not return for the ceremony because I was working fulltime by then.

My background helped me to view with a somewhat different perspective the overwhelming effects of higher education. I was not, for example, too discouraged when, as a sophomore, my undergraduate adviser questioned whether I would even graduate. I also felt that my education had to provide for the possibility of earning a living. I learned much from people I respected and admired, and I also learned from the difficulties and the challenges. If I had not finally succeeded in passing the European portion of the comprehensive examination, it would have been disheartening, and I would have felt that a significant amount of effort had been wasted.

I question those who feel that education somehow elevates one above the rest of humanity. Nor can I abandon ideas and ideals learned earlier unless they are replaced not just by newer, but by better ones. I valued the slower deliberation required to communicate with my handicapped sister, and what I learned from her and from my family stands respectably beside all else that I have learned in life.

This does nothing to denigrate my formal education. I cannot even put into words how much my education and my contact with the people who helped me through it enriched my life. By the time I had finished two years as a graduate student and realized that it was time to leave the university, I also recognized that my education was a tremendous benefit when I began fulltime work in Washington, D.C.

Working at a small, professional, nonprofit association probably does not much resemble the workday in the government offices that proliferated in Washington, or those in large corporations or industrial complexes. One of the elements that was lacking was upward mobility. It was more like being part of a family, and I had had a lot of experience with that. People did the job they were hired and expected to do, or they simply did not remain. I was supposed to move around the office and work with different people at first. Gradually my efforts were focused on the editorial department, and I began to work as an editorial assistant.

The very first manuscript that I was entrusted with editing revealed some of the difficulties of working with authors. My work on the manuscript had been reviewed in the office since, at that time, manuscripts were set in type before authors had an opportunity to see what the editor had done. Then the author received proof copies already typeset. In this case, the author refused to accept most of the changes, and the article had to be almost entirely reset. It was fortunate that this did not happen often, but fortunate for me that the editorial office realized that it could happen to anyone. With the advent of the copying machine, it became possible for authors to see edited copy before it was typeset. I urged extensive use of the copy machine and helped devise systems so that not only authors of articles saw copies of their edited manuscripts, but book reviewers did as well. Computers and fax machines have made the transfer of typed and printed copy faster.

When I began working, my older sister and I shared an apartment in the city that we had to furnish. This began a satisfying period in my life. I liked work, I made friends, and I enjoyed urban life. My sister and I would return to Pennsylvania and maintain our close family ties.

Once my handicapped sister stayed with me while our parents took a brief vacation. My sister's greatest happiness was to be with people, but her speech was not clear. This limited her ability to communicate with those who could not or did not have time to understand her. I had never sensed that she was unhappy as our parents' companion; nor did I sense that they resented her presence in their lives. In truth, I felt that the reverse was true.

She had never, however, had any opportunity to work independently. I asked if she could work as a volunteer in the office during her brief stay. She could try to do some of the more routine work. To help her feel rewarded and accepted, she went to lunch with me and some fellow workers. This may have meant more than money to her since she never mastered the decimal system or realized the value of money.

She made a lasting friend in the man she worked with most, and the box of candy (chocolate, of course) that he sent her every Christmas thereafter had a special meaning for her and, I think, for him. To me, they were both special people at what seemed opposite ends of a spectrum. He was a published author who could appreciate knowing someone for whom writing just a sentence was an effort. Both seemed in some ways "loners," and perhaps that was the common thread.

This was the closest my sister ever came to any type of formal employment. What I had hoped to learn was whether she would be happy performing some kind of routine work over an extended period of time. Somehow, her mind always seemed to function faster than her hands, and she became frustrated with either the routine or her inability to perform efficiently.

Our parents' home was where she was allowed to develop her interests as long as they did not interfere with the lives of others. Teddy bears, television, and music retained their importance in her enjoyment of life. For her, the stability of the home was not disturbed for a number of years. The most significant change occurred as each sister left home. The house and the company of her parents remained the largely unchanged setting that her sisters would reenter at times.

Among the more memorable things that happened during this period were the unusually deep snowfalls that seemed to hit Washington during most of the winters I was there, beginning with the one that fell just before President John F. Kennedy's inauguration. Another left my sister and me stranded in Hagerstown, Maryland, for three days as we were returning from Pennsylvania. Living in any city makes life more difficult when there are heavy snowfalls. These were, however, natural happenings after which life returned to normal.

Other things happened that were to prove more unsettling. Toward the end of this period, during which one of my uncles had been killed in an automobile accident, I was to find out myself how devastating an automobile accident can be. I was driving home from a movie with a friend when our car was struck from behind by another car traveling much faster. The collision pushed us into a parked car. Although the front of my hair was cut, I was fortunate that I did not penetrate the windshield. Most of the damage was to my mouth and teeth, which have never been quite the same.

This was an era of problems related to automobiles for our family. During one of her summer vacations, our youngest sister stayed with my older sister and me in Washington and worked in a department store. As she was crossing the street in front of our apartment, she was struck and injured by an automobile. And, toward the end of this time, a second uncle was killed in an automobile accident.

There were also difficulties related to the apartment. My sister and I were having a Christmas celebration just before leaving for the holiday in Pennsylvania when the kitchen drain in the apartment became plugged. It was a large apartment building, and there were maintenance people. While I was having guests for dinner, the man who was to open the drain arrived. I told him, as he headed for the kitchen, that I had put Drano down, but I was not aware that he did not hear well. He used a professional drain opener, and the mixture of chemicals caused an eruption from the drain just as he was leaning over it to see if anything was happening. His eyes were affected, and no one seemed to know what to do. I suggested that they splash water on his eyes and that the people working with him take him to the hospital as soon as possible. I was later told that washing his eyes with water may have saved his sight, but I felt terrible. In the excitement I also did not realize that my leg had been slightly splashed, and the acid ate through the skin to the bone. For me, the physical damage was minor, but I remember the incident still and pray that the man recovered fully. He returned to the apartment one evening, evidently to confirm for himself that it was just an accident. We talked briefly, and he left. Since I heard nothing more, I must assume that he accepted the fact that it was an accident – one that both of us would have liked to have avoided.

Perhaps it was the different lives we led, or growing stress, that caused difficulties between my older sister and me. Whatever the reason, it became apparent that living together was hurting both of us. When we decided to move to separate places, she remained in the city. I could not afford a place of my own in the city, and so I moved to suburban Maryland and began what I found to be the satisfying experience of living alone. Soon after I moved, however, I did briefly share the apartment with my youngest sister until she found a place of her own.

This change was not easy for either our parents or our handicapped sister. I was awaiting their first visit to my new apartment with some trepidation. Not until my sister walked in did I realize the value of keeping much of the furniture from the old apartment. As she entered, she glanced around apprehensively and then sighed with relief, saying something to indicate that things had not changed beyond her ability to recognize and adjust. This experience may have made future changes easier for her to accept.

Living in the Washington area during these years was exciting. The things that touched the nation seemed almost to be hometown occurrences: inaugurations, beginning, for me, with that of John Kennedy; the death of President Kennedy; the riot following the death of Martin Luther King; the many other political and cultural activities that are part of living in the nation's capital. It never ceased to impress me that I worked about a block from the Library of Congress and not much further from the Capitol.

Work remained as interesting and satisfying as ever. Nothing, however, remains the same. One of my worries had been that my starting salary had been low, and annual increments over five years had been so low that it was difficult to survive in an area that reflected rising government salaries. A change in leadership at the association resulted in recognition and promotion, but a salary that, fulltime, equated with the janitor's rate. Efforts made by the new managing editor to change this were eventually successful, but only for a time.

The Fourth Decade
1966-1976

The word "maelstrom" best describes this decade, for it marked an end to what had been a fulfilling time in my life and destroyed with amazing speed much of what I had anticipated for the future. Among the friends that I had made at work, one had similar interests and educational background and also had family responsibilities that were not yet confining. We enjoyed doing things together, and our friendship grew. Since a close relationship beyond family was new to me, it took some time for me to realize that friendship has limitations, and I had to make those limits clear. This caused some difficulties and almost destroyed our friendship.

At about the same time, the home that I had been enjoying over a three-year period was threatened. One Sunday afternoon there was a knock on my apartment door. There was no way to observe who was in the hallway, and normally I would simply have opened the door. This time, however, something prompted me to ask who it was. The response I got was gibberish. There was no way

I could leave without using that door, and I was frightened. The apartment was on the ground floor with easy access to the outside, something I had enjoyed and never been troubled about. I felt I had little choice but to call the police. They came and searched the area, but found nothing. I left while they were still there. By the time I returned home early that evening, someone had written all over my door. By that time I was really concerned, and I called the police again. Although no one was still at the door, an officer did come. He explained that he was only a short distance away. If I had any more problems, I was to call the police station and try to keep the person talking until an officer could respond. He would come immediately without using his siren.

Later that evening, while talking with my sister on the telephone, there was another knock at the door. She stayed on the line while I answered the door. When I asked who was there, I heard the same voice that I had heard earlier. I asked the person to wait while I said goodbye to my sister. Since she was aware of the situation, she hung up immediately so that I could call the police again. It was not easy to maintain a conversation through a closed door with a person I did not even know, but, true to his word, the policeman arrived in a short time. It appeared that the man had been drinking, and he was taken to the police station.

The policeman cautioned me that the person could only be held overnight and that, since nothing had occurred, it would be best if I did not prefer charges.

The next day I spoke with the apartment manager, and she explained that there were three men in the apartment at the end of the hall, including the man who was bothering me. Since there was only one person – me – in my apartment, if anyone were to move, it would have to be me. This occurred during the fall of the year, never a good time to be looking for an apartment, but I was fortunate to find another one not far away,

The manager insisted that I give thirty days notice before moving, and friends arranged to stay with me throughout that time. I always find moving difficult, but several friends who knew why I was moving offered to help. It made this move much easier than it would have been otherwise.

Just before I moved I went down the hall to say goodbye to the couple who maintained the building. They were the only people living in the building that I knew. They asked me to come in because they wanted to tell me that the apartment manager was involved with the man who had caused the problem. It was risky for them to tell me this since they worked there, but they wanted me to know that they felt that my decision to move was a wise one.

The situation at home finally settled down, but a new supervisor had appeared at work – first a temporary one and then a permanent one. The first of these seemed to be more difficult for my friend to accept, but we survived his brief tenure. The second one made it clear that I would no longer be needed, and I began to look for other opportunities.

My friend, when she learned that I had to leave, resigned her position without telling me. If I had known, I would have tried to convince her to stay, for I knew that it would be difficult for one of us to find work in our field. It would be almost impossible if two of us were looking at the same time.

Since we did not have positions immediately available, we agreed to continue working until either we found positions or replacements were found for us. This time was less than comfortable, but we did our work as we had before. At one point we scheduled interviews in New York City and drove there only to be told that the interviews had been cancelled. No reason was given, and there were no more interviews.

When our supervisor finally found the replacement he wanted, he explained that we could stay as long as he needed us, but he obviously could not keep us on indefinitely. At that point we gave him two weeks' notice. On our last day there, we celebrated with others in the office, and, just as we were about to leave the office for the final time, I received a telephone call from a university press that we had contacted earlier. They had not just one but two openings in their editorial department! We would have to go to the northeast for an interview and move there if we were accepted for the positions.

We were hired. There would be time between jobs if we wanted to take a brief vacation, but we also needed to find a place to live. We visited a real estate agent while we were in the northeast, and, while we were on vacation, he located a two-bedroom flat in a small Massachusetts town near where we would be working. Another move!

I found working with book manuscripts even more exciting and rewarding than I had found the journal. Again I was busy and happy. There were, however, financial difficulties at the press, and I noticed that some people left. I did not realize that this represented the early stages of "downsizing" as it was later to be practiced so widely. When, at a general assembly, the head of the press acknowledged that there had been problems but that they had been resolved and no more people should have to leave, it seemed wise to find more adequate housing. My friend and I pooled our resources and started looking for a house. Homes were scarce in that area, but an advertisement appeared in a local paper that sounded promising. We went to see the house and immediately agreed to buy it since it would accommodate us and our families when they traveled the long distance to visit. The house was in the same small town as the flat where we had been living.

We settled into the house in the spring (another move!) and got to know our neighbors. Again things seemed to have worked out well. By fall, however, we were told that we were no longer needed at the press, and now we owned a house that we had occupied for less than a year.

When we visited our respective families for the Christmas holidays, we told them about our situation. My friend's problems were compounded when the aunt who had helped raise her had to have further surgery for breast cancer. Shortly after we returned from our holiday trip, my friend became ill, but she managed to return to Washington, D.C., to be with her aunt for the surgery. She had just returned to Massachusetts by train when, that same evening, I received a telephone call. My sister, who was also living in the northeast at that time, had fallen down a flight of stairs and broken her ankle. After surgery, she needed a place to stay for a brief time. If I had wondered why I bought a house that I was to own for less than a year, I now had my answer.

While my friend and my sister were both recovering, there was a major snowfall. I knew that I needed to get to work for the few remaining days for which I was to be paid. When the road outside the house was plowed, it closed the driveway beside the house. When I went out to dig the car out of the driveway, one of my neighbors, a young twelve-year-old boy, came across the street to see if he could help. I explained that it was too difficult and too much to ask him to do, but he stayed, and we shoveled until I could move the car. All of the members of his family and others in the area proved to be extraordinary friends considering that we had known each other for such a short time.

Neither my friend nor I succeeded in finding work in the northeast, and I came to realize that owning a house could not determine one's life. We decided to move to the west coast.

The sale of the house was easy. We advertised in the newspaper, and the first person who saw the house bought it, as we had. What was more difficult was to explain to the more than seventy people who called that it had been sold.

My friend went to Washington, and I went to Pennsylvania for Easter. We met at the Pennsylvania Turnpike after Easter and headed west in two cars. The trip was uneventful and would have been pleasant if the future had been more secure. There were floods when we crossed the Mississippi River, but there were no delays on the main highways. I had crossed much of the northwestern part of the country before; now I saw the southwest. The vastness of the interior of this country never ceases to astound me.

My friend and I wanted to find work in the San Francisco area, and we stopped at a motel near the airport, just south of the city. The managers allowed us to use the room as our base while we looked for a place to stay. When we called a rental agency, the response did not seem too promising. Instead, I looked in the newspaper and saw an advertisement for a furnished apartment in the Mission area of the city. The owner agreed to meet us there, and we found that it was well taken care of and offered parking for two cars, which we needed.

If we found work, we could look for something more permanent, and so we did not want to sign a lease for longer than six months. The owner did not feel that a lease would be necessary. It took me longer to find a job, but both my friend and I were employed within six months. Just as I found employment doing what I enjoyed – editing books for professional educators – I received word that Mother was ill. I called my prospective employer and explained that I needed to return east for a couple of weeks. He understood and asked that I call him when I returned. Mother did not recover as quickly as expected, but I did all I could before another of my sisters came to help.

After I returned to the west coast and was assured of employment, it was time to think about moving to a larger, more permanent residence. The newspaper had been so helpful before that I tried to find another home in the same way. The first day I looked I saw a simple advertisement for a two-bedroom flat that had been newly repainted. When my friend and I called about it, the realtor said that the owner did not want to rent to two women. The address was in the newspaper, however, and we decided to look at it anyway. When we saw it, we asked the realtor to try to persuade the owner to change his mind. We explained that we could secure references from places where we had lived before. The realtor must have been persuasive because we were able to rent the flat. After almost six months to the day, we were able to send for the things we had stored in the east. Yet another move!

We had experienced so much change that my friend and I were determined to remain in the flat for some time. We bought a stove and a refrigerator, and we wanted to buy a washer and a dryer, which we were able to accomplish when we received our cleaning deposit from the apartment in the Mission. We knew that we would have visitors, and we tried to furnish the new place in a way that would accommodate them.

We enjoyed living in the city, but I learned that one has to be more careful. On a trip to Fisherman's Wharf, my purse was stolen. After I had replaced the necessary items and had had the locks changed at home, the purse was returned by mail – postage due. The sense of violation remained for some time, but it could have been much worse.

When I returned to the east to celebrate Christmas in 1974, I realized that Papa was not well. I was not completely surprised when I received a telephone call, early in the next year, informing me that he was in the hospital and that the diagnosis meant that he was to have fairly routine gallbladder surgery. What seemed at the time routine soon became catastrophic. Even after surgery, my father remained unable to eat – an essential of life. With the realization that nothing was helping and that his condition was growing worse came the decision to move him to a larger hospital, further from home. Since Mother could not drive an automobile, she and my handicapped sister left their home and occupied a motel room close to the larger hospital in order to be near him. My other sisters and I joined them, in turn, for two-week intervals in order to ease a difficult situation.

My return home was delayed because the bridge that the dentist had put in following my automobile accident some years earlier needed to be replaced. This required a set series of appointments or else rescheduling of the entire procedure. I regretted the delay, but both of my parents felt that I should go on with the scheduled work. The delay meant that my two-week stay fell between the stays of my youngest and my older sister. This proved to be a critical time when my father underwent further surgery to repair an aortic aneurysm.

When I entered my father's room, I was shocked by his appearance, but I dared not show it. His first words to me were, "Your mother and Nora Marie . . . ," but I stopped him. I knew they were his major concern, but I wanted him to know we would manage. We were all hoping that the further surgery would alleviate the problem and that he would recover. He made it through the surgery in spite of a damaged heart, but his heart stopped shortly afterward. Efforts to resuscitate him were successful only insofar as he suffered through the remaining few weeks of his life. I was able to communicate my departure to him, and I left with a heavy heart to return to San Francisco, replaced by my older sister.

Two things stood out during those weeks: the terrible insensitivity and silence in the large and strange (to me) medical establishment and the need to conceal my emotional turmoil, not only from my father but also from my handicapped sister, who reflected what others exhibited. I had a keen appreciation of Mother's almost untenable position, for I could cry only when I was somewhere between my father's room and the motel room. Mother was almost never alone. During the time we were together, we discussed my father's opening words and a future, possibly without him. I could only assure her that there were options.

Less than two weeks after my departure, on May 8, 1975, I received word that my father had died. Precise dates do not often remain with me, but it would be difficult to forget this one. I was calling my youngest sister to wish her a happy birthday. Her husband, who answered the telephone, asked me if I had not heard that my father had died – at the same time the telephone operator was interrupting our conversation with the emergency call from my older sister. I asked how my handicapped sister was doing, and I learned that she had fainted when she was told, but that she had recovered sufficiently for them to return home that same night.

I left for Pennsylvania as quickly as possible. Although the flight was uneventful, I felt that I was moving in a dream. No sooner had I arrived at the airport near home than I was made aware that my handicapped sister was finding the adjustment difficult. She was not sleeping, carefully placing her head against the wooden headboard of the bed to prevent sleep, which seemed to terrify her. My appearance, or more probably her exhaustion, resolved this difficulty almost as soon as I walked in the door. I went to her room and insisted that she put her head on the pillow. She was asleep before I left the room.

It was fortunate that our youngest sister could be home for a time before she joined her husband in Germany. Her presence eased the adjustment, and she also handled business-related matters.

I returned to California with the words "Your mother and Nora Marie . . ." resounding through my head and significant changes looming on the horizon. Soon after I returned, I broached the subject of future plans to Mother. As a way of helping her with the decision, I suggested that she and my handicapped sister make an extended visit to California to see if they might like to live there. She agreed that a visit would be helpful.

The Fifth Decade
1976-1986

Over the Christmas holiday following my father's death, my mother and my sister came for their extended visit. At the time, I was weighing whether it would be better to plan to stay in San Francisco if they should decide to live near me in California. The visit went well, but I did not feel that they could safely make the adjustments that city life would require since they had never lived in or near an urban area. After they returned to Pennsylvania, and much as I dreaded it, I began to face the need to move again – this time to a suburb that would allow greater freedom in a simpler environment.

At the same time that Mother was trying to decide about moving to California, my friend's aunt was also visiting and trying to make the same decision. She decided that she simply could not make the move, and she returned to Washington, D.C. By the spring of 1976, my friend and I found a condominium in the San Francisco Bay Area, but far into the South Bay. The units were intended primarily for people who had raised their families and no longer wanted the care of a house or who simply did not want the expense of a house. Four considerations were crucial in my decision to obtain one of the units: In a condominium, outside care is the responsibility of an association that represents the homeowner, which would allow Mother and me to occupy separate units and spare me what would have been a major effort to maintain the grounds for two homes. Because of the specific purpose for which the condominium had been built, the units were large and had considerable storage. The development was also convenient to shops, the hospital, banks, and other amenities that Mother could use without the ability to drive a car. Finally, the location was a suburban community at the end of the then-new rapid transportation system that allowed me to return to the city at will.

After I was settled, I was in a position to ask if Mother had decided to come to California to live. I knew from previous conversations that she was seriously considering the possibility and was financially able to purchase her own unit, but she wanted to delay purchase until she had visited her youngest daughter in Germany. By fall, she had returned from Germany, arranged to purchase one of the last available units in the condominium, and sold her house in Pennsylvania.

Uprooting after a lifetime of more than seventy years in the same town in which she had been born could not have been easy. The move required great courage and faith, both on the part of my mother and my sister. My friend and I traveled to Pennsylvania in order to drive them back across the country to their new home. The trip, slowed by the 55-mile-an-hour speed limit adopted throughout the nation in response to the energy crisis plaguing the world at that time, was also marred by illness for my sister – an illness that predicted the gallbladder surgery she was to need soon after her arrival and increased my awareness of the responsibility that was now mine.

We got settled in the condominium development, which was still relatively new. The occupants got to know one another as neighbors, which is necessary at least to some extent when people live so close together. We were fortunate in that most of our neighbors shared our desire for neighborliness as well as privacy. Some were older, and time had taught them many of life's valuable and enduring lessons, providing a common bond and a shared concern for each other's welfare without interference. And, having found a parish church where we felt comfortable, we met even more people whose acquaintance we enjoyed, some older and some younger with children.

There was one major problem, however. Soon after my friend and I moved into our unit, we noticed a leak that originated in the unit above. The owner would not allow the necessary repairs to be made, and we suffered water damage over several years before she finally moved. The governing board claimed that they had tried to make the repair and so they were no longer responsible. An attorney, who had been a friend for some time, agreed to handle the arbitration, which we won. The same attorney was to provide much-needed help with other difficulties and confirmed my feeling that it is better to have legal help and advice early to avoid ever going to court.

A single instance that occurred soon after we moved confirmed the wisdom of the decision to move to a suburban area. When I returned from work each day, I would stop to visit my mother and my sister, and my friend and I ate dinner with them once a week. As I walked into their home one evening, I noticed that the telephone receiver was dangling on its cord. I asked why, expecting that a telephone call had been interrupted. Mother said she would explain over dinner, and I can only do my best to re-create the situation.

My mother and my sister had set off for the bus stop on their way to visit the dentist. They boarded the bus and had gone a short distance when Mother discovered that she had left her purse where she boarded the bus. In order not to be late for the dental appointment, she sent my sister off to the dentist and went back for her purse. By the time she got back to the bus stop, the purse was gone. Meanwhile, my sister had proceeded to the dentist's office only to discover that the office had been moved. How she managed it, I am not sure, but she reached the dentist's new office eventually. Mother, upset at not finding her purse, returned home and called the police. Just as the police were bringing my sister home from the dentist's office, mother received a telephone call from the bus company and learned that the driver of the bus immediately following the bus my mother had taken had noticed her purse and taken it to the office. Someone from the office was calling Mother about the purse just as the police arrived with my sister. My mother dropped the telephone receiver to answer the door. Sensing in his telephone conversation with Mother that something was wrong, the man calling from the bus company decided to return the purse himself. He had arrived just before I did, and that is why Mother, understandably, had forgotten to replace the telephone receiver.

I remain grateful to all those who were helpful in this instance and others. Such kindness and consideration seemed to confirm the wisdom of my decision to move to a smaller place where people could still know and care about each other.

My efforts at helping my mother and my sister adjust to their new home had, of necessity, to be limited. What I had told Mother when she was thinking of coming to California still held: No place would be perfect, but we had common interests on which to build. I was at work much of the day, but the nearby shopping area provided diversions that had not been part of their earlier, more rural existence.

I arranged for minor alterations needed in the condominium and for transportation beyond that available for public use. We went to church together regularly and shared trips to grocery stores and larger, more remote shopping areas. We had visitors and toured parts of the state. A pattern did develop.

During the earlier years that they lived in California, my mother and my sister returned to the east for extended visits each year. That was time they shared with my other two sisters, and it was a significant time for them. During one of those visits Mother became a grandmother, and my sister, an aunt for the first time. This was a little overwhelming in that they were alone with my youngest sister when she went into labor, and they had to rely on neighbors to transport her to the hospital. The trips east lasted until soon after the second grandson-nephew was born. Then Mother decided that the journey was too demanding. When they no longer traveled east, I was grateful to my sisters for their visits west. It was not easy for them to take time from their lives. Also, young children frequently do not adjust well to what is different. The two boys amazed me with their concern, consideration, and caring. They occupied an especially bright spot in our lives.

These years were marked by normal everyday activity interrupted by birthdays, holidays, and vacations. It was a rather quiet and uneventful time, but that was not to last.

My work had always meant a lot to me, but that was also to change drastically now. In 1979 my friend and I left fulltime positions to start a small business of our own. We hoped to develop a clientele that could use the type of editorial services we could provide. We set up an office near home – close enough to walk to work. There was no way to know it at the time, but this decision proved almost prescient.

My friend's aunt no longer felt able to maintain her home so we flew east to help her move into an apartment. In a rather short time even that seemed more than she could manage, and we returned to help her move to California. Before leaving for the east we arranged for her to move to a place near us where she could have some care as well as some independence.

I remember the return flight with horror. Airlines had discovered defects in many of their airplanes. The resulting shortage of aircraft made the return to California difficult for us, but, in spite of the best efforts of those who tried to help us, it must have been a nightmare for my friend's aunt. While we were waiting to board the plane in Washington, it was announced that the plane that we were to board had just left San Francisco. It had to get to Washington before it could take us back. My friend's aunt had not been diagnosed in Washington, but we were soon to learn that her illness was terminal.

After the death of her aunt, my friend traveled across the country to contact people we had worked with in the past. When she returned, she was discouraged about prospects for the business, and she told me that she planned to move back to Washington, D.C., a choice that I did not feel I could make since I did not feel that I could ask my mother and my sister to move again when I had no prospect for employment. I had never been sufficiently outgoing to undertake the marketing aspects of a business, and it never developed as I had hoped it would.

Through these years my work life was anything but stable. The publishing industry had always been tenuous. Now it reflected changes brought on by growing automation throughout the business world. Things that had not been possible in communications before entered the realm of the possible, but the effects of the changes were unsettling. Perhaps in an effort to try to find myself and not have a total vacuum in my work life, I undertook the writing of an article ("Help for the Scholar-Author"), which was published in 1982. I continued the search for employment after the business closed, and I found work with a consulting firm that introduced me to editing in the business world.

For the first time in a number of years I felt that I had some permanence in my life and that I could make plans. In the summer of 1985 I noticed that Perry Como was to appear in San Francisco. Since my mother and my sister had both enjoyed his television shows, I obtained tickets. It was simple to reach the theater by public transportation. We had dinner and enjoyed the performance. On the way home, however, we had to change trains. They were crowded, and, in the confusion, we became separated. A helpful station agent managed to reunite us, but the experience made me hesitate to take the risk again. In spite of the difficulties, I am glad we went, for my sense of well-being soon faded.

I had enjoyed my new position editing in the business firm, and they seemed to appreciate my work. In the fall of the year, however, I sensed a change of attitude. On Halloween night of that year I had an accident on my way home from work. The resulting concussion erased any memory of the accident for me. My first awareness came when I awoke in a hospital with a policeman sitting beside the bed. Over time people filled in pieces of what was supposed to have happened. I was supposed to have been speeding and to have gone past a stop sign at an intersection without stopping. Because I could not remember anything about the accident, I could not contest that version, but it would have been very unlike anything I was likely to do. I remain grateful to the policeman, for he took the time to check with people working in the area and could find no indication that anyone had been speeding at the time the accident happened. That charge was dropped, but I had to appear in court even though I was the only one injured. I was fined for going through the stop sign. That allowed the company I was working for to terminate my employment since they did not keep any employee convicted of a "crime." I wonder if they still have that rule. My only comfort was the concern of my family and some of the people I had worked with, as well as help from people where I lived.

Before the accident I had thought about a vacation in Hawaii. After the accident, the need for a vacation became more pressing. Mother recognized this and encouraged me to go ahead with my plans. Shortly after I left, my youngest sister and her two sons came to help Mother until I returned. I thoroughly enjoyed the trip, even though I realized how difficult it would be to find another position when I returned.

I remained keenly aware of my responsibility for my mother's and my sister's welfare and their relative isolation from other family members a continent away. I could never approach a job interview without making that responsibility clear to a prospective employer. Nor could I claim to have mastered the computer at a time when people were expecting so much from it. I had taken a course to learn about computers, and I would have appreciated the opportunity to see how it might have fitted with my past experience and where that might have led. This opportunity never presented itself.

The Sixth Decade
1986-1996

This decade opened, as others had, with great uncertainty. Each morning I scanned the classified advertisements, and I tried to go out to places where I might learn of openings. Unemployment in the area was high, and the experience I had was not in demand. In the absence of employment, I did try again to write something that expressed what editing meant to me, and another article appeared in 1986 ("Editor and Author: A Professional Relationship"). I could still not relocate easily with no promise of employment, for it meant uprooting two households and two other people who could not move readily. Although I could make adjustments in terms of length of commute, relocation became less and less possible. There were some interviews, but none were promising.

As often happens, however, other considerations soon took precedence. Mother had needed the help of an attorney when she first came to California. The friend who had assisted us earlier had arranged Mother's affairs and those related to my sister in a way that kept things stable. Over time, however, I became concerned about Mother's advancing age and what that might mean both for me and for my sister.

This was my first attempt to deal with my sister's disability officially. Our parents had taken the earlier steps required to have her declared legally incompetent, to provide for guardianship rights, to secure Social Security and other legal status, and to guarantee annuity and health benefits through our father's retirement plan – all based on at least one of our parents being able to care for her. Now I was facing the fact that, with one parent dead and the other having passed the age of eighty, my sister had survived one, might survive the other, or might need help beyond what Mother had been providing.

In 1985 I again approached my attorney-friend for advice about the best course to follow. It was suggested that I request a legal conservatorship that would allow me to act for my sister in the event that Mother could not. I was warned that I would be unlikely to secure a full conservatorship, but that, if I could not, then I could request a partial one. I was also cautioned that not every situation is suited to the conservatorship process. I did not, unfortunately as it turned out, know enough to weigh the consequences. Mother and I agreed to proceed with the legal action, and things seemed to move smoothly for a time – to the point of having been assigned a court date.

That was when the state of California, in its effort to protect my sister's rights, sent a court representative to ask her such questions as: Do you understand that, if a conservatorship is awarded, you will not have the right to determine who your friends will be? That you will have no control over your finances? I thought her reply – that we had done a good job so far – was the best possible under the circumstances.

I respect the need to protect people's rights, but neither her mother nor I had any wish to violate those rights. My goal was to be able to continue to care for my sister in accord with Mother's wishes if and when Mother could no longer do so. In some cases, such blunt, tactless questions generate paranoia where perhaps there was none, or increase paranoia if it exists. Perhaps a subtler, more tactful approach could be found. I had specifically requested that my sister not appear in court because I felt that it might be demoralizing for her. She may have been declared legally incompetent earlier, but she was quite capable of understanding the spoken word. She might well have understood what was being said, but, in her context, she might not have been able to understand why it was being said. If the difference could not have been made clear to her, she could have been needlessly hurt.

This report and the impending court action brought my sister to the attention of the regional agency for the "developmentally disabled." I received a telephone call requesting information about her background. The person I spoke with was not satisfied with the information I could provide, assured me that the court date would be delayed until a thorough investigation could be made, and informed me that my sister would have to undergo a thorough psychological and physical examination within a few months of the court action. I tried to explain that she had not come to California until later in life, that she had already been declared legally incompetent in the state of Pennsylvania, and that I did not want her life disrupted to such an extent at this time. They wanted to know how I could possibly presume to know more about her than their trained people would.

It suddenly became clear to me that a "partial conservatorship" meant that we would have to share my sister with the state. And, if we did not feel that the state's demands were in my sister's best interest, then it was doubtful that we could secure protection from those demands. The matter had resolved itself into one quite simple question: If we dropped our request for the conservatorship, could we continue to care for my sister as we had been, without interference? The wisdom of Solomon prevailed: It is impossible to divide a person you love into two.

There was another legal "loose end." When the friend who had shared my home for a time decided to return to the east, I could not afford to buy out her share of the condominium because of the tremendous appreciation in the value of property in California. Mother, recognizing that it would be helpful if I were to remain close, bought out my friend's share. I continued to make the mortgage payments, but it occurred to me that this could cause a problem if my home were to become part of her estate. Mother agreed that it could be a problem, and she resolved it by deeding her share of the property to me.

There are many ironies in life, but one of the greatest must be that the future seldom happens as we had reason to expect that it would. Mother and I had barely emerged from the struggle over the conservatorship when the world that she, my sister, and I knew began to change. It was not Mother's health that brought the change, however. It was my sister's health.

Her gallbladder surgery soon after she and Mother had arrived in California had made me realize that there might be some difficulty in dealing with normal hospital activity. The capacity of any system to deal with difference depends on how much attention can be given to the individual patient, which varies according to how rushed the system is or can become. It can also depend on the obtuseness of the person dealing with the situation. The afternoon after my sister's gallbladder surgery, I had arrived at the hospital to find Mother agitated and my sister obviously uncomfortable. Mother asked me to go to the desk and request something for what my sister said was a headache. Mother had already done this and had been ignored. When I repeated the request, I was told that the only medication they were authorized to give was an injection, and I was asked if I did not feel that this was a little extreme for a headache. My response would have been "no" since I had at times suffered from extreme headaches, but I had learned that you antagonize hospital personnel at the patient's peril. Finally, about a half hour later, a different nurse appeared with the injection and an apology because it was late. The effect was obvious in the almost instantaneous relief visible on my sister's face and in her comment that she felt better "there, too," as she pointed to the incision.

Her inability to pinpoint areas of pain accurately remained a problem. Her care, and Mother's, was the responsibility of the doctor who had accepted the challenge or the need that the circumstances presented and seemed to agree that it was best to keep medical intervention to a minimum.

From the doctor, Mother obtained the name of a dentist also willing to help both my sister and her. Dental hygiene was not, however, something that my sister practiced diligently, especially since she had a strong gag reflex. The condition of her teeth reflected that poor care, and I respected the dentist's concern for her teeth and his ability and that of his staff to relate to her as a person and a patient. When one of her teeth needed to be removed, it was extracted with little difficulty before I learned about it. I called the dentist and explained that it might appear to be the best solution, but I asked whether he had given any thought to how difficult it would be for my sister to adjust to dentures. From his silence, I had to assume that he had not. I was grateful for his patience and understanding, and he waged a small, successful war to preserve her natural teeth throughout her lifetime.

Sometime later I discovered that my sister was becoming hard of hearing. Each time I visited I would find it necessary to turn down the volume on the television set. The sad look on her face made me aware that she could not hear it well at the lower volume. This time her doctor referred her to an ear specialist to ascertain the extent of the problem. Again, she got along well with the new doctor who performed a mastoidectomy to restore her hearing. This experience provided an indication of my sister's strong will. Anesthesia used in surgery can make people ill. I wondered why she was in recovery for so long, but it appears she was fighting not to be ill, and she was not throughout the extended time in recovery. Not until she relaxed in her room did she relax her iron control and throw up – on the doctor!

My youngest sister had arrived for a visit, and we were told that special nurses would not be needed. She and I could have taken turns being with our sister, but, at the urging of the hospital staff, we left. They said that patients frequently do better when family members are not around. I knew that my sister's insecurity was growing, and I was dubious, but, knowing that she was doing well, we departed. I did not ask why they were so anxious to see us the next day when we arrived to take her home. I am sure she was not difficult by her standards, but by theirs . . . . My youngest sister returned home with her sons, and things returned to normal.

By late in 1987, the day after Christmas, to be exact, other physical problems began to emerge. My sister suffered a bowel impaction that required treatment in the emergency room of the hospital.

The immediate difficulty was resolved, but it was while she was at the hospital that I learned she could no longer write even her own name.

Both Mother and I had noticed that life was becoming more difficult for her. Her memory was failing; her speech, never clear, was deteriorating; her ability to concentrate was becoming more limited; her skill in reading was declining. She was reluctant to go outside, and she did not want to be alone. Her sleep patterns were changing, and she was agitated at night.

Mother or I felt a need to be with her at nights until she fell asleep, especially after she began to hallucinate. I had never experienced this, and, with the naïveté born of ignorance, I once asked her if she heard voices. I could not believe the look of tremendous relief that came over her face when she thought that I knew what she was going through. Would that the reed in which she placed such confidence had not been such a weak one!

I began visiting with both Mother and my sister in the early evening, sharing different television shows where each was watching her own set, and I returned at about eleven o'clock each evening to be with my sister until sleep finally came. Sometimes that happened shortly after she went to bed, and sometimes sleep did not come for long hours. This regimen continued for some months.

Early in 1988 I planned to be away through late afternoon and early evening. I left for San Francisco at about three o'clock in the afternoon, after saying goodbye, and I returned at about midnight. I always checked to be sure my sister was asleep, and, with some relief, I noted that she was. Then I went into Mother's bedroom to find her lying across the bed and not too coherent. Since I could not waken my sister or leave her alone, I called the emergency number (911) and explained that I could not communicate well with Mother and that I could not leave my sister. The person I spoke with agreed to send help, and, since the fire station and the rescue people were located just a short distance away, help arrived quickly. The ambulance took Mother to the hospital with instructions to call me when they knew what the difficulty was. By three o'clock in the morning, a nurse called to tell me that Mother had pneumonia and that she would be in the hospital for several days.

When my sister awoke, I tried to explain that Mother was in the hospital, but her sense of reality could not accept Mother's absence. Through the help of friends and neighbors, I was able to deal with my sister at home and Mother at the hospital. I even managed, with some difficulty, to get my sister to the hospital to see Mother, but I do not believe that she ever fully realized that Mother was away or that it was Mother that she saw at the hospital. I would find her talking to Mother's chair at home. It must have been a great relief to her, as well as to me, when Mother again sat in the chair.

Over the course of that year, my sister's health continued to decline to the point where Mother needed help to care for her. A neighbor who possessed the love, the skills, and the interest moved into my sister's life, and we were all grateful.

I then had to make necessary financial arrangements for my sister's care, apart from what Mother was already providing. Again we needed legal help to deal with banks and arrange the allocation of funds that had been set aside in the event that they would be needed. My friend and attorney again performed the type of service that is to me one of the most effective that the legal profession can provide. He helped accomplish what was needed more readily and effectively than I could have managed alone, thereby freeing me to deal with the problems that continued to arise at home.

Mother recovered from the pneumonia, but my sister continued to suffer from unexplained problems – or at least not explained to Mother or to me. I had to respect the doctor's frank admission that he did not know what was wrong. I felt that the effort to find out might cause more complications rather than less, which seemed to be confirmed when even a routine pelvic examination required minor surgery. Clearly we were playing a waiting game, and the struggle was between acceptance and possible remedy for a person who could by then only communicate, even verbally, with severe difficulty. One thing did change: my sister's earlier reluctance to go out transformed itself into an urge to wander. One day I was fortunate to see her walking across the street alone. When I called quietly to ask where she was going, she simply returned home. We had to become more observant and careful, which was complicated because Mother's hearing had become less keen.

Near the end of April in 1989, our world turned completely around. One morning I received a telephone call from Mother, who had found my sister lying unconscious on the kitchen floor, When I arrived, still in my pajamas, I tried to rouse her, but I was not successful. Once again I called the emergency service, and the paramedics responded quickly. They determined that my sister appeared to have had a seizure, had fallen, and had broken her ankle. She started to come around as they picked her up from the floor and carried her down the stairs to the waiting ambulance. I left for the hospital with them – still in my pajamas and a raincoat – because by that time she was terrified. I stayed with her until she was settled in a room.

Then I hurried home to explain the situation to Mother, dress, and return to the hospital where I spent much time over the next several days trying to help my sister adjust to her strange surroundings and help her surroundings adjust to her. What I learned was that, in spite of the very best of intentions, this was impossible. To provide one trite example: My sister, who always insisted on a straw when she was enjoying a soft drink, never willingly used a drinking straw again.

The orthopedist set the ankle the next day and insisted on a full-leg cast. My sister could not put weight on the leg, and the doctor would need to follow her progress. This would have been difficult for someone with good physical dexterity who lived on the ground level or who lived in a building with elevator access. With my sister's limitations and her home on the top level of a two-story dwelling accessible only by stairs, the situation bordered on the impossible. The orthopedist suggested placing her in a "skilled nursing facility."

One instance might go far to show that my sister's care differed from "normal" care. The nurses on her wing of the hospital encouraged us to allow people to write and draw on the cast. I refused because this would have disturbed her sense of order and contributed to her hallucinatory world. Normal people have little sense of the abnormal. I found that some people even fight the need for different considerations. I claim no basis for argument, but I felt that I had some basis for exercising my judgment where there were no clear guidelines.

After serious consideration, I explained to the orthopedist that we were fighting to retain my sister's limited contact with reality. I felt that we would lose her completely if she were removed from familiar people and surroundings. And, apart from her needs, Mother would have found being with her very trying in an institutional setting because of Mother's advanced age. Such a situation would, in my opinion, have been emotionally disastrous for both of them and trying for me in my efforts to meet everyone's needs and expectations both at home and away from home. I had to weigh whether treatment for a broken ankle warranted such dire consequences, and I opted for recovery at home – of necessity my home since she could not use the stairs and Mother could not have managed her care.

Hospitals are anxious to discharge their patients quickly because hospital care is costly. If I had to point to one area of hospitalization that needs to be strengthened as a result, I would have to say that it is discharge planning for home care. In my sister's case, if there was any planning, it was solely for the benefit of the hospital. The patient was not a consideration; nor was her family. If the "planners" had told me that they were going to provide little or no help, I would have done more planning on my own. They were late discharging her, and, when I asked where I could obtain help for her care, I was told that the agency that the hospital normally used required twenty-four-hour notice for evaluation of a case. Sadly, no one had thought twenty-four hours ahead. I was told that the staff would teach my sister how to pivot from the bed to the wheelchair. They did so just before we left, while I was on the telephone trying to secure the services of another agency. If it had not been for the demonstrated roughness in the physical handling of my sister, which was for my instruction and which I felt that I could at least match, I am not sure that I would have had the fortitude necessary to survive what was ahead. And, if it had not been for the knowledge and experience of the woman already helping us with her care at home, I am not sure whether my sister or I would have survived the "discharge."

By the time we reached home and used a rented wheelchair to transport my sister into the condominium and to bed, I still had not found anyone to help me that first evening. It is difficult to believe that the yellow pages of the telephone book proved more helpful than people paid well to know about patient care. I finally located an agency that sent a nurse to evaluate the case and an aide to show me what I needed to know by nighttime since I was with her at night. I did know that I would have to lift her from the bed to a portable toilet with no one to help. Even finding a toilet stable enough for her needs proved to be a problem, and I am deeply indebted to a neighbor who, when she learned of the need, was able to provide one she had used for her husband.

It was fortunate that I was taller than my sister and that she was not large, which allowed me to counterbalance her weight. For the first few nights neither she nor I knew what we were doing, but we managed. The important thing was that she did not bear weight on the leg.

The agency provided help for all evenings and, at first, days on the weekend. The friend who had been helping earlier was there for days during the week. In addition to nights, I eventually cared for her during the days on the weekend. This schedule allowed me to continue to manage the situation in my home and to help Mother. During the afternoons

Mother would come and stay for the evening meal. For a while, it seemed that my home was Grand Central Station. How grateful I was to a neighbor who, knowing that my sister liked macaroni salad, kept us supplied over the months.

Total strangers from the agency came and went until a working balance was achieved. It was difficult to explain to some of the aides that their concern within my home was the patient and that I would retain control of my own home. I deliberately chose not to have live-in people. One of the most difficult areas of adjustment seemed to be whether aides realized that they were neither in a hospital nor in their home.

It did not take long to ascertain which people were better in caring for my sister. Some decided on their own that the case was not for them. One, in particular, wanted to stay because it fit her schedule, but I finally determined that she simply was not the best person for my sister's needs.

To add to the confusion, it is usually suggested that one obtain a hospital bed. I am sure this is good advice in most instances, but I decided that it was not necessary. It was easier for me to make up, and to lift my sister from, a regular single bed. A lift was also provided. Fortunately it did not fit under a normal bed, and a demonstration of its use scared my sister so badly that I had to ask Mother to return that evening to quiet her. The lift was removed the next day.

I did find a restraining jacket that, when tied to the mattress loops, prevented my sister from being pulled out of bed by the weight of the cast should she turn wrong, or from trying to walk if she should waken in the middle of the night and become confused. It did allow movement in the bed, and someone was close at all times. Untying the restraining jacket added significantly to the difficulty of getting her out of bed, and I was relieved when eventually the cast was removed and movement became less of a worry. Then the jacket could be eliminated.

I had expected to have to exert untold effort to keep the bed clean, but I had not allowed for my sister's innate need for cleanliness. I slept in the same room with a light in my face so that I would awaken alert if needed, and, although she could not call me, she rustled around in her bed until I wakened, usually around midnight.

My sister continued to be medicated for seizures in spite of some unpleasant side effects, and this was more or less successful until fall, even allowing the doctor to cut the cast down to more manageable proportions. Then things fell apart again – just about the time that the cast was to come off completely. She had another spell, and the cast was removed while she was again in the hospital. The spells usually occurred late at night, and, being alone, I had to call the emergency people to help and to take her to the hospital. They always impressed me with their quick response, their understanding, their concern, and their skill.

I had learned a great deal from her earlier hospitalizations. This time she was attended by the same people (as "sitters") in the hospital as when she was at home. The number of hours I spent there filling the gaps in scheduling, as well, as the hours I spent helping Mother and keeping things together in two homes made me realize that I would need more help. The illness was no longer a broken ankle; it had taken a new, more serious turn.

I moved from my bedroom, which I had been sharing with my sister, and I looked for people to be with her at night. This time my experience was different: The agency I had used so successfully earlier sent poorly-trained people. An aide I had found independent of the agency proved completely unreliable. The hospital staff insisted that I remove one person provided by another agency for their own reasons, which I was in no position to question. The search for reliable people at night remained a problem. The one thing I knew was that my sister should not be alone, and I filled the hours when I could find no one else.

There were doctors at the hospital who felt that my sister should not be cared for at home, and, deliberately or not, they made our lives more difficult. In one instance it was impossible to obtain the help we needed until it became necessary to call the emergency number again. They again came promptly, and my sister went into intensive care from the emergency room.

By the time I reached the hospital the next morning, the neurologist confronted me. I was told that I could not continue to bring my sister to the hospital with such frequency, that she was terminal, and that she belonged in a nursing facility – all over my sister's bed! I said little beyond acknowledging the problem of frequent hospitalization, but I did reaffirm my conviction that my sister was better at home and that she was attended at least as well there as she could be in any nursing facility.

It was the effect of this confrontation that was more troubling. It made me feel that my sister was not wanted in the hospital, and it made me reluctant to send her there. It took the kind treatment of the emergency ambulance crews, the emergency room staff at the hospital, and those who staffed the units on which my sister was hospitalized throughout her illness to make me realize that she not only had a right to be there, but that she belonged there. Most appreciated our help with her care because they were aware of how difficult it is to provide adequate care for a person who cannot speak or press a call button. Several times we started the drawn-out process of changing her medication and struggling to help her try to walk again, but without success.

When I saw how sick my sister was and realized how sick she was likely to become, I asked our parish priest to visit her and administer the Sacrament of the Sick. At the time, she was passing in and out of sleep, but the priest, who had known her for years and cared about her, realized that he should keep the administration of the sacrament as simple and inconspicuous as possible so that, should she awaken, she would not be alarmed.

Earlier, during a particularly frustrating period, I called my own doctor to try to find someone at the University of California Medical Center who might be familiar with my sister's particular problems. I ascertained that they could work with a responsible internist. Her doctor agreed to proceed in that way, and we moved into late fall.

One time, when she came home from the hospital, my sister needed to be suctioned to ease her congestion. With the help of a skilled respiratory therapist, I learned how to use the machine and helped others learn so that the people she knew could continue to be with her.

This period was the closest I came, during my sister's illness, to feeling secure at night. The doctor approved the services of a nurse who dealt well with the respiratory machine and with my sister at night, until there came a time when my sister no longer seemed to need professional attention. She did so well, in fact, that we again began physical therapy to help her walk. She was overjoyed by the therapist's visits since she truly wanted to walk again. Those times when she was well enough to try, she managed to get from the living room to the bedroom and almost a full block outdoors with help. Her feet needed attention since her toenails had not been cut since her fall months earlier. The podiatrist she had been going to for years arranged to see her on very short notice, and we accomplished one more feat. Still one leg dragged, and the therapist thought the leg might be a slightly different length because of the broken ankle. Measurement showed that length was not the problem, however, and we never knew exactly why one leg dragged.

Either because of the illness, or the medication, or a combination of both, she would at times sleep very soundly over long periods. On October 17, 1989, the day that the third game of the World Series was to be played in San Francisco, Mother, one of the people helping to care for my sister, and I were watching the television set while she slept. Suddenly I realized that we were experiencing an earthquake of unusual proportions. My first thought was to move toward my sister should she awaken and be frightened. The shaking continued for what seemed an extraordinarily long time, and I sat listening for things to fall and break. We were fortunate in that we sustained almost no damage.

My sister opened her eyes for just an instant after it was over, only to fall again into heavy sleep. It was ironic to watch and hear about death and destruction while sitting there looking into the face of death.

The Saturday before Thanksgiving of that year, which was the last time the physical therapist saw my sister, the therapist commented that something had changed. By Thanksgiving Day, my sister was unable to come to dinner – one of the few times she had been unable to do so since she had broken her ankle. We were alone for the holiday, and I fed her dinner in two installments. Mother and I ate afterward, with little sense of the holiday.

My sister seemed to fade steadily then, and, when one of the people who helped at night came, she wanted me to have her taken to the hospital again. Earlier experiences and my sister's seeming inability to recover made me reluctant to go again to the hospital, but the young woman finally prevailed because she said my sister could be made more comfortable. When we arrived at the hospital, they told me that she had developed pneumonia.

Her doctor called me early one morning to get approval to insert a catheter and a feeding tube. The catheter posed less of a problem. Although I felt she would not be happy, I knew it could be easily removed. A feeding tube was another matter, and I told the doctor that I would need to talk with Mother and my other sisters. My own feeling was that I would never be able to explain it to my handicapped sister, and I could not see her accepting it. I called the doctor back after we had discussed the situation to tell him that Mother and my sisters shared my feeling (using much the same logic that had led us to refuse to have a pacemaker installed earlier). I asked if I could see the doctor briefly after he finished his office hours that day, but he was busy.

A young nurse entered my sister's room the next morning when I was feeding her and said that we should have the tube inserted. Then we could throw the food down and not have to worry. I said nothing. In the afternoon two older nurses came in and talked with me briefly. My major concern was whether, if the tube were inserted, it would ever come out. One of the nurses said that opinions varied, but that, in her opinion, it would take a miracle. I preferred to go home and pray for a miracle in my own way.

My sister had almost died in the hospital, and the look she gave me when she again realized where she was seemed to be one of reproach. I asked the doctor to do anything he could that might help her while she was still in the hospital, but not to expect her back again. At the same time I told our priest that I would not pull her back from death again. In one particularly meaningful moment in my bedroom my sister had looked from some small religious plaques above the bed to me and back to the wall, indicating to me that she had faced the possibility of dying, to which she was no stranger based on her earlier experience with our father. The closer death came, the more she seemed to accept it.

In a few more days the doctor arranged her release, and she came home again, by ambulance, for what would be the last time. I met the ambulance at the door, and it seemed that she would not lie back on the gurney because she was afraid that she was not being taken home. The satisfied look on her face as she realized where she was and settled back in bed will long remain with me and bring me comfort.

I know that medicine has accomplished many marvels over time, and modern medicine offers better health and longer life to many. I came through this experience, however, with a feeling that modern medicine can extend death as well as life. Should that be the case, I would opt to live and die as naturally as possible, putting my trust in God. One can only pray that one makes the wisest choices along the way, especially when one must make them for another.

With my sister's return home a little more than two weeks after Thanksgiving, we were entering the Christmas season and facing the dilemma of how to prepare for a Christmas that we might not be home to celebrate. This time there was no question about my sister's coming to dinner or watching television in the living room. She was in bed, and things had to be taken to her. The foods she could eat were limited – apple sauce, clear tapioca made with fruit juice, water-thinned warm cereal, Jello, fruit ices, clear juices – and I made them as needed or made sure that they were available. The food was also used to help get medicine down.

Each day we moved closer to Christmas, and I decided to find a small artificial tree that would fit on top of the desk in the bedroom. I slowly tied red yarn bows on each branch and used cards and other seasonal objects that arrived for decoration, rather than taking time to search for ornaments. A large poinsettia from one of our aunts augmented the tree and brightened the bedroom. My idea was to spend at least some time decorating in an effort to help my sister anticipate the coming holiday.

One day, while I was alone with her in the bedroom, she started to move in the bed, and I was having difficulty discovering the source of her restlessness. As I leaned over the bed, I thought I heard her whisper something. She had not spoken for so long, and it took me a moment to realize that she had said, "I love you." It would have been so easy to miss it or not to understand it. I just hope my momentary delay in understanding did nothing to weaken my response.

If I have conveyed the impression that I cared for my sister patiently and kindly every moment, I would like to correct that impression. The demands placed on me were frustrating, irritating, and at times overwhelming, and I responded at times less than admirably. At one point in her illness, I had to explain this to her in terms of her needs and Mother's. What I knew I did not have to explain was my own unpreparedness and inadequacy. I could do no less than I did; others might well have been able to do more. I can only hope that I provided what best met her particular needs. My love for her prevailed over all. Every decision, every sacrifice, every activity was a response, however adequate or inadequate, to that motivation.

As Christmas came closer and gifts arrived, I was afraid that her pile of gifts would be a disappointment, shades of our childhood, especially since some gifts did not arrive on time. I wrapped things that I would not ordinarily have wrapped so that there would seem to be more when we opened them.

By Christmas none of the women who cared for her or I could move her when we were alone. We were afraid she would slip from our grasp. On Christmas Eve, with two of us there, we managed to move her to the living room to open gifts. Her look of pleasure at being in the living room again was obvious. It was the last time. How much she saw of the gifts being opened is doubtful, but she knew they were being opened. That was what mattered.

On Christmas day there was a vital change. The neighbor and friend who had been with her since before she became seriously ill came over to help, but little could be done. We continued efforts to give her food and medicine, but to little avail. The evening of December 28, another of the women who had helped to care for her since she had broken her ankle and I were with her when she slipped quietly away. In my final attempt at explanation, I told her that I had gone as far as I could with her, but that Papa was waiting.

Then I contacted her doctor, who suggested that I again call the emergency number to secure the help of the paramedics. When they arrived, they spoke with the doctor on the telephone, and then they left without further instruction. I called the mortuary, and after a time the mortician came for the body. Mother and I began preparations for the journey back to Pennsylvania. We were to fly to New Jersey and drive to Pennsylvania with my youngest sister and her sons, where we would meet our oldest sister who would make the necessary arrangements for burial.

Before our plane took off, I walked to where my sister's plane was being loaded, for she was taking her first and last long trip alone. I was comforted only by the realization that, no matter what happened, she would never be alone again. Mother's and my plans moved smoothly in spite of poor weather. My sister's plane was late landing at the airport in Pittsburgh because of the weather, but things finally came together to close the last chapter of her life. Her funeral mass was celebrated on January 2, 1990, in a church fully decorated for Christmas. Vestiges of Christmas still remained when we celebrated a memorial mass in California on her birthday, January 16.

In the early months of 1990 life began to assume a more normal pattern, but that was not to last long. I had asked the neighbor who had helped with my sister for so long to stay with Mother through at least part of each day to help with things that Mother might find difficult. In a matter of months, the woman came to me and told me that Mother had a problem that she did not want me to know about. Much as the woman hated to violate Mother's confidence, she felt the problem was too serious to ignore. She told me about it shortly before Mother was scheduled to see her doctor. Just as we left for the doctor's office and without betraying our neighbor's confidence, I told Mother that she should tell him about anything that was troubling her because, if she did not tell him, she could not expect him to help her.

She was not with the doctor long before he came to the waiting room for me, again over her objections. She had a growth on her breast, and she needed tests and probably surgery. Things moved very rapidly then. At the age of eighty-seven, Mother was scheduled for a modified radical mastectomy – just about six months after her daughter's death. The growth proved to be a malignant tumor, and the lymph nodes were involved. Mother refused aggressive treatment for the cancer. In the time she had left to her, she did not want to be ill. She preferred, instead, to enjoy each of the remaining days of her life, which, at her age, she considered a gift. What she did not want were extended days of agony that might even shorten her life.

Mother recovered well from the surgery only to experience compression fractures of two of the vertebrae in her back a month later. Again, by dint of great effort, Mother traveled the long and painful road to recovery. She was eventually able to leave my home and return to her second-story home, negotiating the stairs with the help of a cane. I had again to bring to the fore all that I had learned from working with my sister, with the added burden of increased awareness. I know that Mother had occasion to wonder about my attitude at times, but at least we could talk about the frustrations and difficulties and share some of the more and less pleasant aspects of what happened each day. Would that I could always have been wiser, kinder, pleasanter, and more understanding, but I was again navigating strange waters.

Some time after Mother's surgery, the doctor she had been seeing for years retired. Mother was never as comfortable with the doctor who replaced him, perhaps because she was much younger than the doctor she replaced and much, much younger than Mother.

Mother rejected aggressive treatment and expressed the desire to remain in her home. I spent many hours there, and in that time we shared an appreciation of the place my sister had held in our lives, as well as a greater appreciation of each other.

I had told Mother when I began a somewhat different version of this work, and the day came when I felt it might be helpful if she were to read it. I hesitated to suggest that she read all of it because I could see her love of reading diminish along with her clear vision and her strength. I was also uncertain how she might react. She read it very carefully and seemed quite satisfied with the result. I especially appreciated the effort because time slipped more rapidly away from her afterward.

I had heard many good things about hospice care. Because Mother had rejected aggressive treatment and preferred to remain at home, that seemed to be a wise choice for care.

For some time Mother required minimal care, and her youngest daughter and her two grandsons, who had been on vacation in the western part of the country, arrived for a visit. It was at that time that Mother's condition worsened, and it deteriorated suddenly and rapidly during their visit.

Perhaps it was because everything happened so rapidly, but the care that Mother was to receive from hospice proved complicated and inadequate. On the day Mother died, it took hospice a long time to respond to our calls. When help finally arrived, the situation improved so markedly that I had to wonder how much better it would have been for Mother if she had not had to suffer through a five-hour wait for the help she needed.

Mother died on July 19, 1991, the day before what would have been our father's birthday – in her own bed, in her own home, and with her family around her. In much the same way that our sister had returned home to rest with our father, now our Mother returned to rest with them.

This is not meant to be a criticism of hospice care. I was given to understand, over time, that the group that Mother's doctor recommended was just getting started, and I can only hope that the letter I wrote to Mother's doctor after her death established that there were problems that needed to be addressed.

I was now facing the last of what seemed the longest ten-year period in my life. I remained in my home and anticipated a quiet time. It was – for a time. At first it was strange to return to oneness, but it could not have been as strange for me as it had been for Mother, who explained after my sister's death that she had never been alone for so long in her somewhat long life. Life seemed to grant me the time I needed to readjust. My sisters helped with their visits. I especially enjoyed a trip to Lake Tahoe with my youngest sister and her family.

By spring of 1995, I received a good report from my doctor late in the afternoon and was walking back to the transit station to return home when I suddenly found myself on the sidewalk. With the help of a bystander I got back to my feet and started back to the doctor's office. Because I could move my fingers, I did not think my arm was broken, but it was. Since I was some distance from home, the doctor who set my arm suggested that I should perhaps consider staying in the hospital overnight, which I did. That same doctor also explained that I could not have simply fallen and broken my arm in the way it was broken. The only other explanation appeared to be that someone must have thrown me to the ground in an attempt to take my purse.

Since I saw nothing and the purse remained on the ground, I could not testify to that.

One does not realize how important each part of one's body is until one has to do without it. I was fortunate that it was my left arm, and I learned to do many things with one arm instead of two. It just took twice as long.

I made every effort to recover from whatever had happened quickly since I had promised to take my two nephews to Hawaii. We had a wonderful cruise of the islands, as I had earlier, and we enjoyed each other's company – most of the time.

Soon after this trip I went to Alaska with my oldest sister. As I told her, we needed to do this before I made one of the last of my major decisions: to move back to the city. I remembered, when I was sitting with Mother during her illness, that I had told her I missed the city at times. She just smiled and said perhaps someday I would go back.

The trip to Alaska seemed to me to be somewhat like visiting frontier America or what I visualize as frontier America, and I truly enjoyed the unspoiled beauty and the smaller communities we visited. In a way it truly did represent a frontier in my life, for I returned determined to make what may be the last major move in my lifetime.

The Seventh Decade
1996-2006

As this decade opened, I asked my younger nephew to help me look around the city for a possible new home. I realized that life for me would soon be different. Challenges, and my response to them, would of necessity reflect advancing age. An awareness that one is getting older comes to those who do not die young or suddenly. Medical advances may extend the number of years a person might live, but modern society does not favor those who live beyond their usefulness. I have found age to be a constant balance between mind and body.

My decision to return to the city was reinforced by the realization that I would not be able to drive an automobile forever. I wanted to be able to use public transportation; to attend church, concerts, and plays; to visit museums, parks, and a library; to shop; and to visit doctors and dentists as needed without depending on others or traveling long distances. I had been unable to do many of those things in my youth and had little time to do them when I was working.

As before in my life, when I have needed to move, the opportunity to achieve this occurred so suddenly that it left me a bit stunned. After my nephew left, I visited a bank to inquire about obtaining a mortgage that would allow me time to sell the home I already owned if I were to find a new one, but not burden me with a debt that I could not handle. Bank representatives preapproved an adjustable rate mortgage that I could pay off early without a penalty. They also provided the names of some realtors who might be helpful. It was the fall of the year, and I felt little would be available before spring, which would give me time to look at some properties and compare prices in an area where real estate was scarce and expensive.

When I visited the first realtor, I saw one brief advertisement for a property that interested me. I spoke with the person who was handling the property and went to look at it. I realized that it was a condominium that as closely resembled the one I was leaving as I was likely to find, which seemed too good to be true. Perhaps this was because the property was in an area where much retrofitting was being done as a result of damage from the earthquake that had occurred in 1989, or perhaps it was because the previous owner had died there that it was still available. Since the construction would be temporary and my sister had died peacefully in my bed, these matters were of little concern to me. The search that had begun in the fall saw me moved into my new home by Thanksgiving and more or less settled by Christmas.

If the suddenness of the move makes it sound easy, it was not. Moving is never easy for me. I had remained friends with the neighbor who had helped me take care of my sister and my mother, and I knew that she had had an even more difficult time afterward. She had taken care of her son until his death at a rather young age, and then she had experienced health problems of her own. When I told her I was going to move, she offered to help me. I was grateful both for her company and for her assistance.

I left only a few things in my old home and had it painted for the first time since it had been built. Early in the next year I put it on the market. I accepted a realtor's lower price guideline, but I insisted that I would not lower the price. I was under no pressure to sell. Many owners in the development, being older, had been forced to sell their homes and, therefore, to accept lower prices. This had reduced the value of units in the development. I was determined to stop this downward trend in the prices in an effort to help other homeowners as well as myself. After receiving a couple of lower offers that I refused, I received an offer that met the set price and, as I had hoped, reversed the trend.

The sale also marked a break with a significant part of my earlier life.

As I had more time to consider my new home, I remembered the prediction of the people who moved me into it that I would not have room for the furniture in the somewhat smaller space. The problem for me was that I had carefully selected much of what I owned and some of the items were gifts or had special meaning for me. I had given away, of necessity, things that I could no longer use. I am not good at planning and measuring for the use of available space; I am, however, reasonably well organized. I managed to keep the items that were moved, and one thing stands out in the effort.

When I started the business that did not succeed, the large table that my uncle had sent to me and that was refinished by my neighbor had to be accommodated. My neighbors had moved to be near their daughter. I called to tell them about my move, and my neighbor's first question was: Had I found room for the table? I was glad that I could tell him that it was in the center of my rather large living area. It is an important part of my everyday life. Many people might not want such a large item in their living area, but it works for me.

Friends and relatives come to the city, and I have made new friends. I have returned to the site of my former home upon occasion, but the passing years have lessened the ties. One of my great losses was the neighbor and friend who had helped me so much. Not only did she move farther away, but she became very ill. I am glad she was able to visit a couple of times before she moved, for she loved the city. And, although I did not drive long distances any more, I drove to her new home to visit with her shortly before her death.

I find myself having to accept the loss of friends and relatives – another sign of the passing of time – along with the maturing of the younger generation. The nephews that I had known as infants and children were now approaching adulthood in a world that seems ever more complicated – perhaps another indication of my advancing years.

When I became settled enough to look beyond my home, I found volunteer opportunities that allowed me to use skills that I had developed earlier, efforts that lasted through much of this decade. One of the opportunities ushered me through an awareness of the growing importance of the computer.

The computer has become as omnipresent as television became when I was younger. I simply have not found a need for one in my life. I recognize advantages, but there are also complications that others seem more willing or able to handle. I rely on the newspaper and television for news reporting, the telephone for instant personal communication, the mail for less urgent matters, and a short walk to use a copy machine for exact reproduction or a fax machine for rapid transmission of text. I still enjoy reading the newspaper, books, and magazines for pleasure, and I find reading on a computer screen taxing over time. I acknowledge that my attitude would not be appropriate if I were involved in business or doing research, but I do not see my needs changing at this time of my life. What I did not see to such a large degree with the development of television is the tendency toward isolation of the individual that laptop computers and cell phones have produced. It is somewhat disconcerting, when walking down the street, to have to wonder whether the people one passes are talking to you, to themselves, or to someone else.

One aspect of my life did, as always, remain stable throughout the confusion of moving. Although I changed churches when I moved, God's home, as always, has remained a stable influence wherever I find myself. I had volunteered for years at the church I had left, and I felt that there would be no need for me to do so in the large city church close to my new home. That did not prove to be the case, and I became a volunteer at that church and also for the diocese of which that church was a part. I undertook the diocesan work with a friend whom I had met at a symphony concert, and the work strengthened our friendship.

All of these volunteer activities required the reading skills that I had developed over the years, and I enjoyed them and the people I met through them. Toward the end of the decade, however, I found myself tiring of the long automobile trip and the hours that one of the volunteer opportunities required. The organization was also changing the tasks to a degree that was uncomfortable for me, and so I decided to cease that effort. I gave up driving a car at the same time.

The first church that I attended when I came to the city was located at the top of a high hill. It became more difficult for me to climb the hill, and it was not convenient to use public transportation to reach the church. I was able to find another church, also at the top of a hill and further away, but public transportation made the journey much easier. Now I know that I can attend mass for as long as I am able.

I maintained my volunteer efforts for the diocese, although I could no longer drive my friend to the site. We continue to enjoy each other's company at lunch each week, for I walk to her home. In time my efforts were no longer needed there, either.

Volunteering remains as a possibility, but, for the moment, I need the time to care for my own affairs.

People often verbally reward volunteer efforts, but many do not realize how much energy such efforts require. Such efforts can be ignored, changed, or no longer needed, but it should be recognized that such efforts, besides being a gift, can be burdensome. Volunteering requires time, skill, and dislocation from the familiar of everyday. If those efforts are no longer needed, appreciated, or become burdensome, it is best to change one's focus.

I celebrated the fiftieth anniversary of my graduation from high school with the members of my class later in this decade, the passing of time becoming ever more apparent. But the passing of time does not mark the end of time. I look forward to tomorrow, and, although I know it will be different, each day still has its pleasures that I hope to enjoy to the fullest and its problems that I hope to resolve in the best way I can.

These considerable changes in the routine of my life in my later years have proved welcome. It was my awareness of the passing of time that prompted me to plan a trip to Europe that I had never been able to take earlier. The planning took almost a year because I hoped that my two remaining sisters, my brother-in-law, and my two nephews would be able to accompany me. They did, and the trip met all of my expectations. Because I now realize that it would be difficult, if not impossible, to achieve the same result again, I appreciate the trip even more. I also learned that I must continue to use air travel when it is necessary, but air travel is no longer a pleasure for me.

My perspective is changing. It has become less planning for the future and more an appreciation of the present. I try to care for my physical and logistical well-being in ways that will allow me to enjoy my remaining years for as long as possible.

Because dental problems that originated with the automobile accident in the 1960's were resurfacing, I arranged for more extensive procedures that I hope will not have to be done again in my lifetime. In trying to get to the dentist's office for what was to be an unusually long appointment, a young woman rushed past me pulling a suitcase on wheels. She succeeded in getting around me, but I did not see the suitcase. I tripped and injured my right hand. I did make it to the dentist's office for the appointment, and the dental work has proved successful. It took a longer time to recover the full use of my hand, and, although it may never be quite the same, I am happy that I can still write, type, and play at playing the piano – just not as easily as before.

I still see the world through glasses, although the ophthalmologist feels he could change that if I wanted him to operate. I have cataracts on both of my eyes that do not yet seem to affect my vision. There may come a time when he will have an opportunity to try. Until that time, however, I remain grateful that I continue to see as well as I do, and I remain ever grateful that glasses allow me to do that.

Apart from these rather minor difficulties and the aches and pains that seem to come with age, I have good health that allows my independent living. Supported by routine annual visits to the same doctor I have been seeing for many years, my health will, I hope, last as long as possible.

As knowledge of the world continues to grow, my world becomes smaller. Movement requires more effort, and I tire more easily, which makes me appreciate more what I can still do. My life has been blessed, and I am grateful.

Afterword

I still remember the earthquake that occurred in the Bay Area in 1989, but that was a disaster over which one had no control. It was much more difficult to cross over into a new century and a new millennium and face an even greater catastrophe created in the mind of man. It was the idea of flying airplanes filled with people into buildings filled with people in the middle of heavily populated areas, as well as other devastating occurrences deliberately planned. History is full of accounts of man's inhumanity to man, but it is still difficult for me to understand such acts. I regret the time and the resources that have been lavished on armed conflict, not to mention the loss of lives, but the wars (Korea, Vietnam, the Persian Gulf, the Middle East, Iraq, Afghanistan, African nations) go on.

These are not, however, the only unnatural threats facing the modern world. Much of what transpires is subject to economic and business practices that harm both individuals and the environment. Improved means of communication, beneficial as they are, have also moved problems beyond their local import to national and even international significance.

The world seems smaller because news from all parts of the earth and beyond is almost instantaneous, which makes things seem to happen faster, with little time to adjust. Just knowing what is happening is not always helpful unless one can do something about it. Perhaps we need to take some time to think about remedies for problems that exist and to improve things we already know about before embarking more speedily into the unknown or growing so large that there is no accountability. Can a country, or a business, or a religion that fails to help its own people or to resolve catastrophes, scarcities, or crimes against humanity set itself up as a model? The clay feet of leviathans eventually appear. Or, am I, once again, just getting old?

I look back on a life that seems filled with change. I ask myself what things have given me courage and satisfaction to make the most of each day. Since life begins with those one depends upon most, I was fortunate to be part of a caring family.

I organized this work based on a quote from Dietrich Bonhoeffer, but I turn now to my parents. Both were concerned with providing and preserving strong family ties – my father because his were less strong, and my mother because hers were stronger. If family ties are to last, however, they require reciprocity.

I still remember my father enumerating the three things he felt were most important in life: God, country, and mother, in that order. If I were to make any change in my experience of those three things, it would be to broaden them.

Within my family, and as part of childhood, I was able to develop a strong faith that was tested but survived. That faith was augmented, throughout life, by an education that moved, from the day I was born through public school, and on through the university, with a focus on the study of history as a way to orient life in the present. My faith continued to grow, even as my world expanded. And, since faith must move from rote learning in childhood to acceptance in maturity, I have always been grateful for the opportunities I have had to develop my gift. The God of my childhood encompassed my whole world of faith.

My approach to country has been in the more minor role of responsible citizen. Although I do not support armed conflict, and I continue to hope for a lasting peace, I thankfully recognize the greater sacrifices that some citizens make. That is why, as long as people are dying for this country, I prefer not to demonstrate in a way that could weaken our country and cost more lives. I consider the right and the obligation to vote the single most influential act that any citizen can perform, with the broadest possible consequences.

Now I come to the last of the things that my father considered so important: mother. I broaden "mother" to "family," for I am confident Mother would approve. And I further broaden "family" to include those, whether related or not, who have cared about me. Without those people, my life would not only have been harder; it might well have been impossible.

When I finished school, my work advanced my learning and provided friends and acquaintances that shared common interests. Lack of employment also provided lessons and burdens as I moved into a period of caring for others that allowed me to learn more about myself. As I said earlier, I was motivated to set forth these memories in the hope that they might say something to those who, in my opinion, are facing the more complicated existence of the present day.

The most important lesson I learned through life was that, if I made the most of each day, the future seemed brighter. Now, as I face the later years of life, I am looking forward to using each day as I have in the past. The future still looks bright, for there is much to do as I have the time and the energy to do it each day.

When I first decided to write a book, it was to be a biography of my sister, Nora Marie. Over time I was persuaded that it would be more helpful to show how her life influenced mine. I still hope that the original intent has not been lost. I still hope that:

> some who read might understand,
> some might learn,
> some might appreciate,
> some might know,
> some might hope,
> some might love,
> some might endure,
> some might pray, but
> none should despair.

With these thoughts in mind, I dedicate this book to Nora Marie, and I thank all–relatives, friends, and acquaintances–who have contributed so much to my life.

Then there are those who have helped make this book a reality. I especially value the efforts of James Mullen, who taught art at the State University of New York at Oneonta, in depicting the passing of time.

I also appreciate the help and advice I have received from Rita Walljasper, also an editor, who shared proofreading chores, as well as the efforts of those at the California Publishing Company who turned the typewritten manuscript into a book.

The memories are mine alone, and, as I said earlier, the memories of others, even those close in time or space, might differ. I have tried my best.